be your best

sally gunnell chronology

1966	Born in Chigwell, Essex.
1973-81	School sports, including gymnastics, long jump, sprinting, volleyball and netball.
1982-83	Focused on heptathlon. Competed at senior level.
1985	Changed to 100m hurdles.
1986	Commonwealth Games in Edinburgh; won gold in 100m hurdles.
1988	Seoul Olympics 400m hurdles; placed fifth.
1990	Commonwealth Games in Auckland; won gold in 400m hurdles, silver in 100m hurdles. European Championships in Split, Yugoslavia; placed fifth in 400m hurdles.
1992	Barcelona Olympics; won gold in 400m hurdles. Bronze in Relay. Married Jonathan Bigg.
1993	World Championships in Stuttgart; won gold in 400m hurdles and broke World Record (52.74s).
1994	European Champion in Helsinki; won gold in 400m hurdles. Commonwealth Games in Victoria, Canada; won gold in 400m hurdles.
1996	Atlanta Olympics; 400m hurdles semi-final – pulled out due to injury.
1997	World Championships in Athens, retired due to injury.
1998	Finley born.

be your best

GET FIT

LOSE WEIGHT

BEAT STRESS

BUILD CONFIDENCE

sally gunnell

with kathryn leigh

Thorsons

My thanks go to Steven Purdew and the team at Forest Mere, the fabulous setting for many of the photographs in the book; to Cotton Traders for supplying clothing and Forza for giving us Reebok fitness equipment.

Thorsons

An Imprint of HarperCollins*Publishers*

77-85 Fulham Palace Road

Hammersmith, London W6 8JB

The Thorsons website address is: www.thorsons.com

First published 2001

10 9 8 7 6 5 4 3 2 1

© Sally Gunnell, 2001

© HarperCollins *Publishers* Ltd, 2001

Sally Gunnell asserts the moral right to be

identified as the author of this work

Photography by Robin Matthews

A catalogue record of this book

is available from the British Library

ISBN 0 00 710777 3

Printed and bound in Italy by Rotolito Lombarda

contents

about the authors

Sally Gunnell OBE is one of Britain's most successful and popular athletes. She is the only woman in history to have held four major titles concurrently: Olympic, World, European and Commonwealth plus the world record in the 400m hurdles.

She retired from the track in 1997 and now works in a number of fields, including athletics coverage for the BBC, motivational speaking and ambassador for the Millennium Youth Games. She lives in Sussex with her husband Jon and son Finley.

Kathryn Leigh is an established fitness journalist. She is the Contributing Fitness Editor for *Health & Fitness* magazine and her work has appeared in *Zest*, *Shape*, *Men's Health*, *The Daily Mail* and *The Sunday Telegraph*. She enjoys running near her home in South East London and sporadically enters triathlons with her husband, Neil.

meet sally gunnell
the power of a personal best

Ever since I won the Commonwealth 400m hurdles, people have written me letters asking for advice or have come up to me on the street for a chat. They share themselves with me, and I share myself with them. For a non-stop chatterbox, it's great!

At first, people asked me about running and athletics. Then, after I retired from the track in 1997, they started asking more general questions to do with wellbeing. How could they look after themselves better? What's the quickest way to budge a few pounds? Why did they always feel tired? How could they exercise when they never have time?

I helped as much as I could in a single letter or a five minute chat, but it bothered me that a few quick tips would only scratch the surface. Under the simple questions, there often seemed a strong sense of dissatisfaction which boiled down to one thing: weight. Being overweight cast a shadow over their entire lives. They felt sluggish. They couldn't do everything they were supposed to. They were defeated, as though they'd let everything go. Frumpy feelings had the power to stop them developing their relationships, career or self-esteem. Since they had no sense of achievement in their daily lives, their dreams were obscured or forgotten.

This book contains all the information I wished I could pass on to people when they stopped me in the street. It's a recipe for pure energy, with all the motivation and scientifically-based tips you need to get the fat off and become fit and energetic again.

elite versus ordinary

Can an Olympic athlete really understand what it's like to feel frumpy? You bet! I've never been completely happy with my body. At school they called me Grasshopper – I had a short body, long legs and knobbly knees. (Spending so much time at long jump probably didn't help.) By the time I was 18, my physique was best described as roly-poly. By 1986, I was a stone and a half over my ideal weight and I worried about it constantly. These days, despite the medals, I still think my stomach sticks out and my torso is too short. Plus I'm not half as toned as I used to be – luckily I don't have to run around in a leotard any more!

I've had plenty of physical ups and downs but after a while I discovered that no matter how my body changed, what really mattered was confidence. Confidence is the biggest word out there – if you're a confident person, the world is your oyster. If not, the fun and joys of life can slip by without you.

We're often given the impression that if we lose weight and get fit, confidence will magically happen. There were times when I'd done both those things, but still wasn't very confident. Eventually, I learned only one thing made me feel truly happy and outgoing: reaching a personal best

My idea of a personal best has changed along with me. Back in 1984, when I was 18, it was making senior trials for heptathlon. In 1990, it was Commonwealth gold. Two years later, it was winning Olympic gold in Barcelona. Then in 1993, I won gold in the World Championships and broke the world record   that, for me, was an ultimate dream come true. Now, my personal best lies in different directions. My husband Jon and I have a two year-old son, Finley, who we want to raise with all the happiness, fairness and security two loving parents can provide. I also have a range of professional commitments, from athletics coverage for the BBC to motivational speaking. I want to do the best I can in all these roles and each time I do a little better than before, my confidence grows.

Everyone has a personal best to strive for. It might be raising your kids right, becoming a company MD or running a 10k road race. It might be something you've always wanted to do but lies dormant inside you, either forgotten or unexplored. Whatever it is, reaching your personal best will improve your confidence and self-esteem. Each time you win through, it reinstates in your mind that you can do it, regardless of the odds.

can fitness really change your life?

I believe it can. It gives you a sense of control. It proves to yourself that you can do something off your own bat. This in itself is a positive move, and the good feelings compound as you tone your heart, start to feel healthier and get the endorphins pumping.

Fitness is all about what you can do, unlike diets, which tend to focus on what you can't. Forget about rules and restrictions; being fitter gives you more freedom and more options. Once you start, you can reach a new achievement every week. Each time you discover, 'Yes! I really can do that!' your confidence grows a little stronger and you're a little closer to being your personal best.

I've presented the information as an eight week training programme. This is enough time to make many positive changes and see great results, but it doesn't have to be the end of the story. Once you feel the difference a small amount of exercise can make to your entire life, you'll probably want to make it a permanent feature. If you do, the achievements will keep growing, along with your confidence and zest for life. I've never found anything as satisfying as beating my own personal best – you win every time.

take your

starting

blocks

Before you know where you're going, you need to know where you are. Fill out these questionnaires to assess your current activity and eating patterns; it's the first step to thinking how you could improve them!

how active are you?

You might be busy, but are you active? Like most people, you probably think you're reasonably active – take a few minutes to work it out and you might be in for a surprise.

WHAT TO DO

Below is a list of activities. For each 10 minute session you do of each activity per week, put a mark in the appropriate column. Choose either:

GENTLE   you do it at a pleasant pace which makes you slightly warm;

ACTIVE   you become warm, slightly out of breath or your muscles tire slightly;

SPORTY   you sweat, pant or really push your muscles.

For example, if you do a 20 minute run on Tuesday, put two marks (two lots of ten minutes) in the 'sporty' column. If you do an hour's vigorous housework on Thursday, put six marks in the 'active' column. If you stroll through the park on Sunday for 40 minutes, that's four marks in the 'gentle' column.

Foot Work

	GENTLE	ACTIVE	SPORTY
Strolling			
Brisk walking			
Power walking			
Hiking			
Jogging			
Running			
Other			

Swimming

	GENTLE	ACTIVE	SPORTY
Breaststroke			
Front crawl			
Aqua aerobics			
Other			

Cycling

	GENTLE	ACTIVE	SPORTY
Mountain biking			
Road cycling			
Other			

Class Exercise

	GENTLE	ACTIVE	SPORTY
Aerobics class			
Boxing (class or punch bag)			
Circuit training			
Dance class			
Group cycling class			
Martial arts			
Pilates			
Step class			
Tai chi			
Yoga			
Other			

Gym Workouts

	GENTLE	ACTIVE	SPORTY
Elliptical trainer			
Indoor rowing			
Stationary cycling			
Ski machine			
Step machine or stairclimber			
Treadmill			
Weight training			
Other			

Recreational Activity

	GENTLE	ACTIVE	SPORTY
Canoeing			
Clay pigeon shooting			
Dancing			
Hang gliding			
Horse riding			
Kayaking			
Night clubbing			
Orienteering			
Paint balling			
Paragliding			
Rock climbing (indoor or outdoor)			
Rowing			
Sailing			
Skating			
Skiing			
Sky diving			
Sub-aqua diving			
Surfing			
Wind surfing			
Water skiing			
Other			

Domestic

	GENTLE	ACTIVE	SPORTY
Gardening			
House cleaning			
Laundry			
Lawn mowing			
Playing with children			
Shopping			
Other			

Sports

	GENTLE	ACTIVE	SPORTY
Badminton			
Basketball			
Baseball			
Bowling			
Football			
Golf			
Netball			
Rounders			
Squash			
Tennis			
Triathlon			
Volleyball			
Other			

Now add up the marks in each column and work out how long you spent at each level of intensity.

GENTLE: [ ] hours [ ] minutes

ACTIVE: [ ] hours [ ] minutes

SPORTY: [ ] hours [ ] minutes

WHAT DOES IT MEAN?

Government guidelines recommend at least 30 minutes of activity almost every day. If you already clock up this much 'gentle' or 'active' exercise, well done, you keep things ticking over.

However, to improve your body shape and energy levels, your body needs the stimulus of 'sporty' levels of exercise. The more intense your activity, the more calories you'll burn and the sooner you'll notice the benefits.

For this eight week programme, I recommend three to four hours a week of 'sporty' (or at least 'active') exercise. Don't worry if you're currently on zilch – once you get some ideas from the Get Physical section, you'll be able to build it up at your own pace.

what pushes your excitement button?

Exercise shouldn't be awful/boring/pointless/repetitive. None of these activities are, but they'll all improve your fitness. Go down the list and tick the the box which applies to you.

Foot Work

	HAVE TRIED	DO ALREADY	WOULD LIKE TO TRY (AGAIN)
Power walking			
Hiking			
Jogging			
Running			

Gym-Based Exercise

	HAVE TRIED	DO ALREADY	WOULD LIKE TO TRY (AGAIN)
Aerobics class			
Boxing (class or punch bag)			
Circuit training			
Group cycling class			
Martial arts			
Pilates			
Step class			
Tai chi			
Yoga			
Weight training			

*Right: Many different activities can benefit your fitness –
the second you find activities that you enjoy*

Swimming

	HAVE TRIED	DO ALREADY	WOULD LIKE TO TRY (AGAIN)
Breaststroke			
Front crawl			
Aqua aerobics			
Spring board diving			

Sports

	HAVE TRIED	DO ALREADY	WOULD LIKE TO TRY (AGAIN)
Archery			
Athletics			
Badminton			
Baseball			
Basketball			
Bowls			
Fencing			
Football			
Golf			
Hockey			
Netball			
Squash			
Tennis			
Triathlon			
Volleyball			

Recreational Activity

	HAVE TRIED	DO ALREADY	WOULD LIKE TO TRY (AGAIN)
Ballroom dancing			
Canoeing			
Ceroc dancing			
Clay pigeon shooting			
Croquet			
Clubbing			
Conservation work			
Folk dancing			
Hang gliding			
Horse riding			
Ice-skating			
In-line skating			
Kayaking			
Mountain biking			
Orienteering			
Paragliding			
Road cycling			
Rock climbing (indoor)			
Rock climbing (outdoor)			
Rowing			
Sailing			
Scottish country dancing			
Skiing			
Sky diving			
Sub-aqua diving			
Surfing			
Water skiing			
Wind surfing			

Have tried: If you've marked eight or more, well done, you know the possibilities. If you've marked less than eight, that's fine too, because you've got a whole new world to explore!

Do already: If you regularly do three or more activities, great – you're cross training. A mixture helps with motivation and results. If you do less than three in a typical fortnight, you could benefit by increasing the types of activity you enjoy.

Would like to try (again): These are the activities which press your 'excitement button' and make your tummy flutter with possibility. Picking up a new sport does wonders for your weekly exercise programme, giving it a focus and results you can look forward to using. For every 'would like to try', refer to the back of the book, where I'll tell you how to get started.

are you eating enough?

I bet your immediate answer is a big, 'Yeeeesss!' You're more likely to worry about eating too much than not enough, but to change your body with fitness, you need to give it four-star fuel.

Write down the number of times you've had a reasonable serving of each of the items listed on pages 14–15 in the last week:

This programme isn't about strict diets and deprivation. I want you to enjoy food as much as I do, but I'd like you to make educated choices about what you eat. Although this isn't a full list of healthy food, everything on the list is good for you (until you add lots of butter or creamy sauces – we'll come to that later).

If you eat something from each section every week, it's good that you're familiar with a wide variety of foods. If a couple of sections are distinctly lacking, why not look up some of the items in a recipe book and find out how to use them?

If you eat more than 20 different items every week, you eat a good range of foods and are therefore more likely to absorb the vitamins and nutrients you need for health. Fifteen is good but any less and you've got some exploring to do!

Healthy food definitely isn't boring – look at the huge variety of flavours, colours and textures in the list. The recipes and food section later in the book will help you bolster the number you enjoy every day.

Remember, everyone should have at least five good portions of fruit and vegetables a day. How many were on your list?

Bread

Brown

White

Wholemeal

Rye

Crispbread

Other (eg ciabatta, pitta)

Potato

(portion = one medium
or two small)

Baked

Boiled

Mashed

Beans & pulses

Baked beans

Black-eye beans

Butter beans

Red kidney beans

Chick peas

Lentils

Rice, grains & pasta

Brown rice

White rice

Pasta

Couscous

Bulgar wheat

Polenta

Noodles

Cereals

Bran flakes

Cornflakes

Fruit & Fibre

Muesli (not toasted)

Shredded Wheat

Porridge

Weetabix

Very large fruit

(portion = one 100g/4oz
slice or 1 cup)

Honeydew melon

Mango

Water melon

Medium fruit

(portion = one)

Apple

Banana

Grapefruit

Nectarine

Orange

Peach

Pear

Small fruit

(portion = two)

Apricot

Clementine

Kiwi fruit

Satsuma

Tangerine

Plum

Very small & dried fruit, berries

(portion = a handful)

Blackcurrants

Blueberries

Cherries

Dates

Gooseberries

Grapes

Prunes

Raspberries

Sultanas

Strawberries

Vegetables

(portion = 2 serving spoons)

Artichoke

Asparagus

Aubergine

Avocado

Beans (fresh)

Bean sprouts

Beetroot

Broccoli

Brussels sprouts

Cabbage (red, green or white)

Carrots

Cauliflower

Celery

Chinese leaves

Corn

Courgettes

Cucumber

Leeks

Lettuce

Mushrooms

Onions

Parsnip

Peas

Peppers

Spinach

Swede

Tomato

Watercress

Fish, meat & dairy products

Chicken breast

Turkey

Lean meat (not fried or minced)

White fish (eg cod, brill)

Oily fish (eg haddock, tuna in brine)

Shellfish

Quorn

Tofu

Fromage frais

Cottage cheese

Low fat natural yoghurt

Skimmed milk

take your starting blocks

15

meet the be your

personal

best team

Before you commit to an eight-week programme of exercise and lifestyle change, I expect you'd like to know if it works! It does – but you don't have to take my word for it. I invited five people to test it for me. They're of different ages and backgrounds, and I hope one of them has a situation or problem which is similar to yours. That way, you can follow the extra tips and advice I'll be giving them throughout their training programme.

be your best

Name: **Alison Creasey** Age: **26**

Commitments:

I'm a groom for show jumping horses and own a yard with my boyfriend, Chris. Each day brings different demands – as well as the day-to-day running of the business, I have to arrange and attend competitions. We're often at home for only three or four days a week and it can mean late nights and early mornings.

What's the problem?

I used to eat everything and not put on any weight but a few handles have recently appeared. I always thought my work kept me quite fit but it's clearly not enough to keep the weight off any more.

Diet and exercise habits:

My job means I ride horses for two or three hours a day and do a lot of lifting and walking. Breakfast is a couple of slices of toast or a fry-up if I've been working in the rain. Lunch is usually a salad, pasta or sandwiches. In the evening I have meat like chops, chicken or stew and two servings of vegetables.

The problem is junk food, especially while we're away. I nibble a lot on crisps and chocolate – often four or five bars a day!

I smoke 15–20 cigarettes a day. I'll give up eventually but for now, I enjoy it.

Goals:

I want to be more toned. I'd like to work on my legs – I think my bum and thighs are quite fat.

Name: Lucy Batham-Read Age: **31**

Commitments:

I'm the general manager of a software house. I visit clients in London three days a week and work from home two days a week. My husband, Richard, and I have a baby daughter, Ella, who is cared for by a nanny while we're at work. We also have two dogs.

What's the problem?

Before I had Ella, I exercised four or five times a week. I tried to keep going to the gym after she was born but it was too much to fit into a day. It's been hard to get rid of the extra weight – I'm still in the same clothes but they don't feel as comfortable, especially around the thighs and bottom.

Diet and exercise habits:

I'm lucky to have the dogs, because I have to take them out morning and evening for 30 minutes. Once a week I jog instead of walk, sometimes pushing Ella in her buggy.

I eat cereal when I get up at 6:30am (Ella's an early riser). If I'm working from home, I have an apple and toast or some biscuits mid-morning and a sandwich at lunch.

I control my eating much better at home than the three days when I'm out and about. I often have lunch with a client and order a two- or three-course meal. Then on the way home, if I stop for milk or bread, I seem to end up with a bag of biscuits as well. I nibble them in the car and in the afternoons when I work from home.

In the evening, I often eat crisps while I wait for Richard to come home. For dinner we have pasta or jacket potatoes, salad or a few vegetables. I don't think we eat enough vegetables, so we try to juice as well. I drink a couple of glasses of white wine a week.

Goals:

I want the muscle definition back in my arms so they look good in summer, and to slim down the tops of my legs. I tend to build muscle easily so I don't want them to look huge. And the good old stomach – I had a flat stomach before Ella and I've been shocked by how hard it is to get back.

be your best

Name: **Karen Gayler** Age: **34**

Commitments:

I'm the mother of Curtis (5) and Reece (3). I look after them three days a week and spend two days doing the accounts for our family business, a busy hardware shop. My husband, Ryan, works there full-time and helps me care for the kids at the weekends.

What's the problem?

I haven't been very impressed with my body since I had Curtis. It's never been fantastic but two caesareans have taken their toll on my stomach area. My energy is very low, so by 9pm I just want to have a bath and hop into bed.

Diet and exercise habits:

I don't do any exercise. Maybe once a week I walk my son to play group which is 15 minutes, but mostly I take the car because of time. I've tried swimming, aerobics and running but lost motivation or felt too self-conscious to stick at it.

When I'm at work I eat very healthily, with soup or a sandwich for lunch, pasta or salad, no cakes or biscuits. When I'm with the kids I might have crisps, or if I meet friends I'll have a cake or ice-cream. If the kids have an early meal and don't eat it all, I can't scrape it into the bin, I eat their leftovers. I share a bottle of wine with Ryan after the kids go to bed, probably three or four nights a week.

Goals:

I want to be slimmer in the middle area – stomach, bottom and thighs. I'd love them to be a bit smaller so I can fit into some of my old clothes.

be your best

Name: **Neil Perrin** Age: **38**

Commitments:

I'm a partner in a firm of chartered surveyors. I work in the London office three to four days a week, and spend the other day or two driving to inspect possible sites for development. My wife, Sue, and I have three children, James (9), Sophie (7) and Emma (4).

What's the problem?

I don't get enough exercise. I'm a member of a gym and aim to go three lunch times a week, but usually end up going only once. In the last couple of years, as my position has become more senior and I have more pressure at work, my physical condition has really slipped. I'm getting big around the tummy.

Diet and exercise habits:

When I go to the gym, I usually do 20 minutes on the treadmill, 10 minutes on the elliptical trainer and 15 minutes on the weights machines. I ran the London Marathon two years ago and trained three times a week plus a long run at the weekend, but knee problems mean I couldn't do that again. I play golf every other weekend and race around taking the kids to tennis, football or parties.

For breakfast I have a bowl of cereal and a glass of orange. Lunch is either a chicken sandwich or twice a week I have a business lunch with beer or wine. I can't resist a few handfuls of peanuts when I get home. For dinner we might have pasta with tuna or chicken pie with vegetables and a couple of glasses of wine.

I enjoy food and can eat a huge amount. Sue and I try to eat out once a week and if she leaves half a meal, I'll finish it. I'll probably have a starter and a main course, rather than pudding, and quite a few drinks.

Goals:

I want to lose about a stone and regain my running fitness. My test is walking up the escalators on the underground – it used to be easy but now it's hard work. My upper body needs toning as well.

Name: Pam Grant Age: 54

Commitments:

I work three days a week in a doctor's surgery. My two children, Sam and Matthew are grown up and live away from home. My husband, John, and I have a big garden which I like to keep in pristine condition.

What's the problem?

Without changing my lifestyle or eating habits, I've put on a stone and a half in the last three years. I assume it's to do with the menopause. I've got friends who are the same age and we're all gaining weight for no apparent reason. It makes me feel sluggish and unattractive.

Diet and exercise habits:

I've gone through phases of exercise all my life. For a while it was squash, now I belong to a tennis club and play twice a week. It doesn't make me feel puffed or fatigued though. I belong to a gym but never go.

I used to ride a push bike everywhere but that was years ago. I think it's still in the shed but probably not in very good condition. My gardening varies from just an hour a week to whole days at a time, depending on the season.

I've tried to be more careful with my diet recently. Breakfast is toast and marmalade but I skip it on the days I have to get to work. Then I get the munchies by 10am, and have two or three biscuits with my morning coffee. I have four cups of tea or coffee during work, and a few biscuits with each one, plus another three cups of tea at home.

At lunch time I buy a pasta or rice salad and a roll. In the evening I have something like a baked potato or spaghetti bolognese with fruit for pudding.

I don't drink alcohol but I smoke 10 cigarettes a day. I know it's not doing me any good and I'd like to give up.

Goals:

I want to lose the weight I've gained in the last couple of years, especially around my stomach and backside. I want to make more of my gym membership and stop smoking.

motivation:

the secret

to life-long

fitness

I have every faith you can reach your personal best, whether it's a gold medal or simply to enjoy living inside your skin. Whatever you want, you can do it. Of course, changing your body takes some commitment; you have to stay active and think about your eating patterns — we'll come to that soon. But believe me — those are just frills compared to the one thing which will really make it happen: Your mind.

What's the one thing which separates the world's top athletes from achieving a gold medal? The mind. What's the one thing to make you choose the sofa over a 20 minute jog? Your mind.

It's certainly not your body, because bodies thrive on movement. That's what they were designed to do — you're even rewarded with a free buzz in return for doing it (endorphins are the body's gift in return for treating it well). No, it's that tiny, roguish part of your brain that pipes up when you need it least. For me, it's usually first thing in the morning, when I'd planned to put on my trainers and fit in a run before breakfast. 'Hold on, you're too tired,' it argues. 'See those slippers? They look much more comfy. Put those on and have some hot toast instead. The run will still be there tomorrow.'

It takes real effort to override that voice and put my trainers on, even though I know a quick jog will make me feel good for the rest of the day. No matter how many promises you make to yourself and all the obvious reasons for regular activity, that tiny but vocal part of your mind can sabotage it all in a flash.

Luckily, that part of your mind is still part of you. That means you can control it. I learned how, and I'm going to show you too.

First, you have to believe the mind is an incredible tool; all you have to do is pick it up and use it. Correctly, that is! Too many times, I've seen people pick up their minds like a big, powerful hammer but instead of using it with care and precision, they grab the wrong end and start beating themselves with the handle! 'You'll never get a medal at this rate,' they tell themselves. 'You're just not good enough. Everyone else has trained ten times more than you so you'd better pull your finger out if you don't want to look stupid.'

I've met caring, sensitive people who have used the same clumsy method for weight loss. 'Look at this great, flabby stomach. It's disgusting! Right, no cakes, no biscuits, no chocolate, not a single thing until it's flat.' They then convert delicious food into little parcels of fat and protein, into must nots, can't haves and no ways. It's not that they lack motivation to reach their final goal, some want it so desperately they spend their waking lives worrying about every morsel. They just need to find a way to make their motivation work for them, not against them.

Let me explain why I believe in the power of the mind so completely.

barcelona 1992: a world class mind-game

Ten months before the 1992 Olympics in Barcelona, my chances of winning a gold medal looked slim. I'd come fifth in the 1990 European Championships when everyone had me pegged as favourite. Now, they said I wasn't tough enough to win. They said I was the wrong colour and the wrong build. Clearly, I was no sleek cheetah – I was short, with more tendency to go plump than develop big muscles – and it would have been so easy to accept their predictions.

Luckily, their negativity just made me think, 'Right! I'll show you!' Instead of quitting, I searched even harder for advice on preparation. I visited the 1968 Olympic champion of the 400m hurdles, David Hemery, to find out how he achieved his magnificent victory. He told me to visualize.

'Oh, I do that already, the night before a race,' I told him. 'I go through it all in my mind so I'm mentally prepared.'

'No, I mean really visualize,' he said. 'Every day, several times a day, I want you to go through every aspect of the 400m hurdles Olympic final in your mind, from the instant the gun fires to moment you cross the line. I want you to imagine every possible race. I want you to stand next to every possible competitor, with different athletes ahead at different stages. Only one thing must always be the same: you must always win.'

Luckily, their negativity just made me think, 'Right! I'll show you!'

So I did. Every day, eight or 10 times a day, I went through that race in my mind. I did it while I ran; I did it lying down with my eyes shut. Sometimes the imaginary me made a mistake, so I'd see myself correcting it and carrying on. Sometimes I'd nearly get to the end and find I wasn't in front, so I had to rewind and play it again to make sure I was. I must have run that final more than 2,000 times before I lined up for it on a warm evening in Barcelona.

I was so nervous I wanted to be anywhere else in the world but there. I left my coach in the warm-up area and then, for about 45 minutes, I sat in a room with the other competitors, all trying to psyche each other out. As we walked onto the track I could feel thousands of people watching us but I didn't look up. I just kept thinking to myself, 'Okay Sally, this is your chance. You really can win this. This is your moment.'

We went to our starting blocks. There was more waiting around but I just wanted to get it over. A whistle blew, to warn us to get ready. My heart did a double beat and suddenly I had a strong feeling like I'd never had before. 'You're going to win this,' it said.

That was it. I don't remember anything of the race. I knew I'd crossed the line but had I really won? Or was this just another mental practice? I didn't know if I was going over it in my head or

I'd actually done it for real. I had to keep saying to myself, 'You've done it! You're an Olympic champion!' I was in a magical cocoon and I couldn't take in everything, the stadium was a sea of British flags and people waving. When I saw my family and heard them say it, I finally knew it was true. I really had done it.

Seventy per cent of that race was won by my mind. From then on, I was totally sold on mental techniques and I continued to learn more about their potential. Visualization is not a magic potion you can only use once and never again, it's the ultimate 'use it or lose it'. The more you practise, the better it gets, as I found a year later, before the World Championships.

cold war at the world championships

This time, the odds were stacked a little differently. I had won every race leading up to the event in Stuttgart and I was a firm favourite, so the pressure was intense. My preparation had been thorough, I was ready to do my best and then, with one week to go, I came down with a terrible cold. I have trouble breathing through my nose at the best of times, so this was a double whammy! I felt tired and depleted, but worst of all I felt all my confidence drop away. I was on antibiotics and nowhere near a hundred per cent. I considered dropping out before I even arrived but the event was so important I decided to run the heats and see what happened.

I got through my heat, through the semi-final, qualified for the final and didn't actually feel too bad. With a rest day before the final, I decided again to rely on the power of my mind and convince myself I could win. Every moment of that entire day, I spent going through that race in my mind. It wasn't easy. You know that roguish voice that tells you how good a sofa looks? Mine was particularly busy that day. Every time my mind drifted it would take the chance to pipe up with negative comments. 'You'll never do it,' it said. 'You're not well. You may as well give up.' Well, everyone has their opinion but you don't have to agree. Before it could finish a sentence, I'd catch that voice and say, 'Shush! I'm a winner! I can do this, absolutely!'

The next day, all the finalists went through the same process of warming up, then sitting in a room together, waiting to be called. I sat there trying not to cough because I didn't want any of my competitors to think I was anything less than fearsome. Over and over, I told myself, 'You can do this. You can do it!'

And did I? You bet. Not only did I come first, I broke the world record with a time of 52.74 seconds. So no matter what your goal is, whether it's a gold medal, or a slimmer, healthier you, trust the power of your mind. You can do it.

take responsibility for you

Before any wonderful, long-lasting changes can take place in your life, you have to accept just that: this is your life. It's your responsibility. The buck stops with you. This might seem tough but it's also liberating. It's an amazing power and one which we too often give up in order to blame someone or something else. 'My coach didn't come through for me.' 'My mum's fat and I've got her genes.' 'When I arrive home I'm so hungry I have to eat biscuits.' 'I'm too busy to exercise.' 'I'm sure it's a medical problem which stops me losing weight.'

It's very easy to think like that, and that's where so many people fail, in athletics and in normal life. A personal best wouldn't be worth having if you didn't have to work for it, so you can expect to face many barriers. You have to either move them aside or find a way over them.

I've always been very determined – or is it stubborn? – when faced with a barrier. Even when something looks impossible, I tell myself, 'There's got to be a way!' When a travel agent told Jon and I we couldn't possibly reach a European fixture in time, I gathered all the flight timetables and pored over them myself, thinking, 'There's got to be a way!' It drives Jon mad sometimes, but it's better than accepting early defeat.

Every time you surrender your responsibility and pass it onto someone or something else, you make yourself impotent. When you recognize the buck stops with you, you regain the power of choice. Either you do something about it, or you choose not to do something about it. Just accepting the decision often makes the consequence easier to bear.

If you don't believe me, look at amazing athletes like Ludmilla Engquist, the Swede who won gold in the 1996 100m Olympic hurdles. In 1999 she discovered she had breast cancer and her right breast was removed. If she'd chosen to give up athletics at that point, the world would have respected her decision and she could have retired, satisfied with her achievements. Instead, she chose to train full time through her chemotherapy and raced at the World Championships in Seville later that year, where she sensationally won bronze.

> **The way I see it, life deals everyone certain cards. You can't choose them but you can choose how to play them, and you can make that choice any time, any place, at any point down the line.**

You can start right now if you want, by choosing to accept responsibility for yourself. Just say something like this in your mind: 'My lifestyle is my business. I am fully responsible for how I live. It's not up to my genes, my family, my income or the weather, it's up to me. I accept this responsibility and I thrive on it.'

motivation

take responsibility for your inner voice

Right, let's sort out that roguish voice, that little chatterbox sitting on your shoulder. If it's like mine, it watches everything you do, just waiting for a chance to dive in and let you know how much you've messed up.

Psychologists call it the inner critic, and believe it or not, it's on your side. It's meant to protect you by telling you how mediocre you are before anyone else gets the chance and really hurts your feelings. Unfortunately, we often let it spiral out of control and it starts telling you things you wouldn't say to your worst enemy. 'You'll never win.' 'You're such a fat pig.' 'Missed your workout again, well that's no surprise.' How mean can you be?

Luckily, that voice is yours, so you are totally able to control it.

I learned to shut mine up in a couple of weeks. First I had to stay alert for whenever it piped up, which was more often than I'd realized. Then I had to be ready with an instant interjection, which told myself how great I was. (Yes it does feel silly at first, but it's no more outrageous than telling yourself how stupid you are.) Over a short time, my inner critic got the message and started quietening down, and now I say many more positive things to myself every day than I do negative. If you're going to think anything, you may as well make it positive.

If you have problems shushing the unfounded nonsense which comes from your inner critic, here's a couple more techniques to try:

◆ Put a handful of paper clips in your right pocket first thing in the morning. Every time you think a negative thought, move one paper clip into your left pocket. If you end the day with a pile of paper clips in your left pocket, you'll realize how harmful this is and want to do something about it. The physical movement also acts as a wake-up call if you don't realize how many nasty things you say every day.

Be Your Personal Best team-member Karen said she could be hard on herself, so I asked her to do this for one day. 'I put 500 paper clips in my right pocket and was quite impressed that by the end of the day, I'd only moved eight. Maybe that shows I expected myself to be worse than I really am, which in itself is a negative thought! It's still eight more than I need, and doing this showed me when they were most likely to pop up.'

◆ As soon as you have a negative thought, write it down. Something like 'My God you're fat!' is cruel and hurtful when you say it to yourself, but write it down and it looks so ridiculous it's almost funny. Have a good laugh and its power will instantly vanish. I bet your inner critic will think twice before saying something so dumb again.

TAKE RESPONSIBILITY FOR YOUR REACTIONS

Here's one of the most liberating things I've ever realized: Every person has the power to decide how they react. Don't you think that's incredible? Let's say you stick to an exercise plan for a week, then a project blows up at work and you have to miss several sessions. You have a choice. You can feel angry or resentful, hating the person whose incompetence caused all the extra work. You could even feel guilty and blame yourself for not fitting in everything. Or, you could accept that this is a temporary situation and look forward to next Tuesday, when you're sure you'll be able to start again.

Or say you eat at a great restaurant and go to town on the dessert menu. I'm well known for this – many years ago, I would have gone to bed feeling gruesome and hopeless, cursing myself for failing in my diet. Not any more. I might feel lethargic the next day but I never feel guilty – I thoroughly enjoyed my banoffi pie and I make no apology for it! I just make sure to eat normally for the next few days so it balances out.

The point is, how you feel is up to you. If one thought process makes you feel terrible, while the other makes you feel a bit better, why choose to feel terrible?

If your emotions tend to get the better of you – especially the negative ones – an analytical approach can really help. If I had a bad training session or things really weren't working out, I'd sit down afterwards and try to work out why. Whatever's happening, there's got to be a reason. If you're not getting the results you wanted, don't feel mad or disappointed. Assess your progress and try to work out why. Have you set your first goal too high? Have you given it enough time? Are you really doing what you need to reach the goal?

Don't give up – there's got to be a way. At the very least, give yourself a pep talk. Say, 'Yes but at least you can run five minutes longer than you could two weeks ago!' Acknowledge how hard you've worked and tell yourself how great it will be when the improvements start coming again.

There are many things in life we can't control. If you can't change the world, you can at least change your attitude towards it.

TAKE RESPONSIBILITY FOR YOUR LANGUAGE

Cynicism is pretty cool these days. We're supposed to be street savvy, to expect the least and not be surprised when promises are broken. So many people said I'd never win gold that if I'd listened, I would have put my trainers in the bin long ago. It's good to know that this is another choice: either I can choose to go with the cynical flow and give up my dreams because they're all impossible anyway. Or I can be brave, trust the power within me and go after my goals regardless. I love this saying: It's better to try 100 things and fail half of them, than try one thing and get it perfect.

TAKE RESPONSIBILITY FOR THE FOOD YOU EAT

Have you ever opened your mouth and found a Mars bar inside it? And wandered around the house thinking, 'Wow, that's incredible, how on earth did that happen?'

No, nor me. If I ever find a chocolate bar in my mouth – as I sometimes do when I'm feeling run-down or tired – it's because I've chosen to put it there.

I've heard some incredible excuses where food's concerned but really, it all comes down to you. Food does not have a brain. It does not have a voice. It does not have a hypnotic, evil spirit and it does not call you from the kitchen, saying 'Pleeease, come and eeeeat meeeee.'

When you take responsibility for your life, take responsibility for the food you eat too. If biscuits or cakes or a Twix end up in your mouth, don't act all surprised. Don't get thoroughly depressed, either. Just admit, 'Right, I'm having this because I really want it and I'm going to enjoy it.'

By the same token, don't eat them if you would really prefer not to. Just don't. My worst temptation time is around 5 o'clock, when I make Finley dinner and everything looks so tasty. I know I'm not really hungry though, so I tell myself if I'm that starving, I'll eat something from the fruit bowl first. If I can't look an apple in the eye, I know I wasn't really starving after all, so it's easier to wait until I'm ready for a proper, nutritious meal.

goals, affirmations and visualization

I was never one of those athletes who decided at the age of six they wanted to win Olympic gold. When I changed my training to focus on hurdles in 1985 I was a secretarial office-worker who trained part time and had a distant dream of making the Olympics. However, all my career, I've set myself small, achievable goals and progressed step-by-step, until even my dream goals were in reach.

Every self-help book out there will tell you how important it is to set goals. Just as you'd be foolish to get in the car without knowing where you're going, you'll never reach your lifestyle destination unless you know what it is and how to get there.

I highly recommend that you take a few minutes now to decide where you're going. What do you want to achieve with this programme?

Did you say lose weight? Gotcha! This is one goal I'd like you to reconsider.

My friend Pete Cohen is a fitness trainer and sports psychologist who devised the *Lighten Up* programme of weight loss. He says having the goal, 'I want to lose weight' is a bit of a dud. For one thing, it focuses on the exact thing you want to get rid of: weight. And whatever you focus on, is what you get. For another, it's miserable! Why not come up with five new goals which emphasize the happy, positive side of keeping fit and looking after yourself?

Here's the type of thing I mean:

I want to run for 30 minutes non-stop

I want clearly defined biceps

I want to enjoy a 10 mile walk with my family

I want to do 25 press ups without stopping

I want to complete my first triathlon within six months

I want to eat fruit for morning tea

I want enough energy to play with my kids at the end of the day

I want to stick to this exercise programme for eight weeks

Goals work best when they're specific, so you know exactly what you're aiming for. They should be measurable, such as '30 minute run' '25 press ups' or 'every day'. It helps to give yourself a time frame, such as 'within four weeks.' Your goals should also be realistic. If you've got an Olympic medal in mind and you haven't started training yet, well, fair enough. Make that your 'dream goal', think about it often but break it down into immediate goals which you can achieve within a couple of months. Every time you reach a goal, celebrate! Then give yourself a new goal and look forward to completing that too.

While you're writing your clearly defined goals, come up with some 'affirmations'. They're statements you say to yourself as fact, even though they might not be true – yet! The great thing about the human sub-conscious is that it doesn't actually know what's real and what's not. So if you imagine something hard enough, your lovely brain will assume it's true and before you know it, you're half way to making it real.

Here are some sample affirmations:

◆   I am healthy and slim

◆   My body is strong and beautiful

◆   I feel great when I finish triathlons

◆   I love the taste of crunchy apples

◆   I turn heads when I wear a sleeveless top

◆   I have tonnes of energy

◆   There's enough time in the day for everything

◆   I have strength inside me to stick at this exercise programme for eight weeks!

To make your affirmations even more convincing, regularly close your eyes and visualize yourself being the person in your affirmations. Give the picture as much colour and detail as you can muster and sincerely believe it is real.

I know from experience this works, and it was proved by an American study too. Researchers tested two teams of basketballers. The first team practised free-throws on court. The second team simply laid back and imagined practising their free-throws. The result? The court-based group improved by 24 per cent, a great result, but the visualization group did even better, with 25 per cent improvement!

That's why, after all those visualizations, I finished my Olympic final not knowing if it was real or not. That's also why you have to put a stop to that negative chatter box, because you'll quickly believe the nonsense it spurts is true.

So, don't worry about pounds, inches or any aspect of weight loss. Concentrate on your happy, attractive goals and affirmations, follow the programme, take care of yourself, and let weight loss happen as a brilliant, natural bonus.

respect your body

Have you ever seen a book on human anatomy? The way our bodies fit together is astounding. Around 650 muscles, 206 bones, 60,000 miles of blood vessels, assorted cartilage, ligaments, skin ... thousands of tiny pieces all creating a mobile home for who we are and what we want to achieve. Sometimes I look at my feet and think, 'Wow, all the pounding they've taken and they still work perfectly.' You can push yourself to the limit one day and wake up, ready to do it again the next. It's miraculous.

Yet most of us give our bodies a bad rap. When I asked the Be Your Personal Best Team what bit they liked best about their bodies, there was a lot of umming and aarring:

- ◆ 'My stomach is quite flat. It never sticks out but it's not very toned.' (Alison)

- ◆ 'I wouldn't say I've got one but I suppose people remark on my eyes.' (Lucy)

- ◆ 'Maybe my arms – some people's get fat and flabby but mine aren't too bad.' (Karen)

- ◆ 'My legs. They need firming up, but I'm basically happy with them.' (Neil)

- ◆ 'I don't particularly like any of it. My legs, I suppose. They're not brilliant but I prefer them to the rest of me.' (Pam)

True, they all came up with something – but they managed to put themselves down in the same sentence too!

No such problems when I asked which bit they liked the least: 'My bottom and thighs are a bit large. If I put on a skirt or trousers, it sometimes looks a bit rude.' (Alison)

'Hips and thighs – they need a lot of work.' (Lucy)

'My legs – they're too short, with fat knees. I hate wearing skirts or shorts.' (Karen)

'My tummy and chest, both of which are a bit wobbly.' (Neil)

'My stomach and backside frustrate me. I'm sick of them.' (Pam)

Okay, so some bits may not be as gorgeous as the bits we see in the magazines, but it's still an incredible, working whole, which always tries to do its best by us. That's right – your body is on your side! It does the best it can to ensure your survival. Although we're all blessed with certain genes and body types, much of its appearance is a response to the stimulus you give it. So again, take responsibility for your lifestyle and don't blame perceived shortcomings on anything else, not even your metabolism!

Once you gain some appreciation for the intricacies of your body, I hope you'll be less inclined to mistake it for a garbage can. If you're full before you've finished a meal, don't keep stuffing. Would you smear half a spaghetti bolognese over an incredible masterpiece in an art gallery? No! So give your masterpiece a break and use the bin instead.

the 'too busy' conundrum

The single most common reason for not exercising is, 'I don't have time.' The best intentions quickly skew under pressure and my roguish voice is certainly loudest at the start of a busy day. Let's face facts – we're never going to have bags more time than we did yesterday. If you honestly want to commit to an exercise programme, your attitude has to change first.

How do you see exercise? Is it an indulgence? An extra? Just another demand on your precious time? Wrong. Exercise is a serious investment in yourself which pays dividends faster than any life insurance policy. Study after study has shown people who exercise have stronger immune systems, so they're less likely to need time off due to illness. They have better concentration, they're more productive, they have better morale and even if they take out an hour a day to exercise, they still achieve more overall.

Besides, if you don't look after yourself, what will happen to all these responsibilities? They'll go down the pan, because you're too stressed, tired or ill to look after them properly. Your needs deserve to be looked after as much as anyone else's.

Find your own favourite time of day for working out. For me, it's first thing in the morning, because I feel as though I've achieved something and can look forward to the rest of the day. For our case study Neil, it's lunch time. Or it would be if he gave exercise the priority it deserves.

'I start the week meaning to go to the gym three times but I'm lucky if it's once,' he says. 'By midday, I'm so busy I usually think I'd better stay at my desk and get my work done. I could work 24 hours a day, six days a week and still have things to do, so leaving for half an hour at lunch time is quite difficult.'

He could look at it that way. Or, he could admit that if the work's always going to be there, it won't make much difference if he nips out for 50 minutes. His colleagues should respect him for being assertive and managing his time well.

If, like Neil, your main commitment is work, you could use your lunch times too. Join the gym closest to your work or go for a jog. If you don't have showers, bring a towel and have a wash in the basin – sweat doesn't smell bad unless it's on the skin for a few hours. Avoid a timetable which makes you go home before you go out to exercise – that sofa is a commitment killer.

If you have a busy schedule, book the time into your diary in indelible ink, so it's there in black and white. If someone rings at the last minute and tries to take that slot, tell them sorry, you have an important meeting at that time. Well, you do!

Even Neil managed to visit the gym regularly when he trained for the London Marathon a couple of years ago. That's because he knew a serious goal was on the horizon, and he'd have been in big trouble if he didn't invest the time. Let's face it, with our sedentary life-styles, we'll all be in trouble if we don't invest the time, but more to the point, we'll be missing out on life. Yes, life! Never forget that the life you're living now counts just as much as the life you'll have when you're rich, famous or retired. This is it! So spare yourself a little time to enjoy it by meeting your fitness goals and investing in yourself.

Exercise doesn't have to be taken in one big chunk to count. Research shows you get the same effect, whether you take an hour's continuous exercise or four sessions of fifteen minutes throughout the day. Maybe you can fit these little bursts around your daily tasks? A brisk walk to work, a 20 minute jog at lunch time, 10 minutes of press ups, lunges and squats while dinner's cooking, 10 minutes energetic play with the kids, 10 minutes of rope skipping in the garden ... it all adds up.

If your main commitment is family, try to get them involved in activity too. That way you all get the benefits. Sometimes I come home having been out all day and want to spend time with my little boy but know I need to fit in a training session too. He goes in the pushchair, I get the dogs and we all go for a power walk – that's three jobs rolled into one! We have a baby seat for when we go cycling and kiddie back-packs for hiking. Fin loves it as much as Jon and I do. I've also chosen a gym with great crèche facilities; some have kids' clubs for older children.

Remember, kids with active parents are far more likely to be active themselves, so do it for their sake as well as yours.

getting past the honeymoon

The first four weeks of an exercise programme or lifestyle change usually aren't that bad. In fact, it's quite exciting to do new things, experience new sensations and maybe see some early improvements. The hard work starts once the novelty wears off, so it's important to keep your interest up.

I recommend a training log. It can work as a planner and a diary in one – you fill in your intentions for two or four weeks at a time and note down after each session what you achieved and how you felt.

It will help you to spot any patterns, like the type of workouts you enjoy most or if you're consistently finding them too hard and need to ease up a little. At the very least, it's a great buzz to look back every few weeks and see how much you've improved.

Introduce variety into your routine. Experiment with different ways to exercise – very few people get a kick out of 20 minutes on the treadmill followed by 20 minutes of weights, time after time. Mix up your activities, go for different times, work at different intensities, go to different places, work out with different people ... there's no excuse for boredom.

I had very clear objectives with my training – coming top in the world! – and all the training I did had more focus because of it. Working out twice a day, six days a week was less a chore than a challenge when I could see where it would take me further down the line.

Always choose something you enjoy. I couldn't have done it for 15 years if I didn't love it. Maybe you could use your weekends to develop a new interest, such as rock climbing, wind surfing, tennis, kayaking, cycle rides with the family or trail running, and let it become a focus for your training sessions during the week.

Develop a store of activities you can call on depending on how you feel or how busy your schedule is. If I've planned 45 minutes of resistance training and really don't feel like it, I swap in a swim or a jog and do the resistance work later in the week. Or sometimes I just bite the bullet and get started – tell yourself you can stop after 10 minutes if you really don't like it and odds are, once you get going you'll enjoy it too much to give up.

If all else fails, the car breaks down, the cat falls sick, you're up against every deadline and you just can't fit in your planned session, don't worry. Try for a ten or 15 minute brisk walk just to keep everything ticking over.

turn a major disaster into a minor set-back

Let me tell you more about that awful race in 1990. For seven months, all I'd thought about, all I'd trained for was the 400m hurdles European Championships. I'd won gold at the Commonwealth Games a few months before and I was favourite to win this. I felt confident and as we lined up for the final, it seemed everything would go my way. The gun went off and I ran hard but something was wrong. When it came down to it, I just couldn't produce the power I needed. Although every fibre of my body was pushing hard, it felt like I was standing still.

I finished fifth. I should have at least won a medal – I probably should have come first! I left the track crushed, with my head down and in tears.

At the time, it seemed a major disaster. I couldn't have imagined a worse outcome. But a girl can't cry forever, and once the dust settles there's only one thing to do: find out what went wrong and make sure it doesn't happen again. That failure made me think about my entire set-up. The Commonwealth Games in January meant I'd missed my basic winter training. I needed to do more strength work to last the full 400m. I needed more rest between training sessions. I had to make time for a regular massage to prevent injuries. I needed advice on diet and visualization. With the power of hindsight, I'm certain that disaster in 1990 was instrumental to my success in 1992 and 1993. It caused me to reshape my entire training regimen and made me fitter, stronger and more confident.

No matter what goes wrong in life or in your exercise programme, learn from it and move on. Try to find ways to prevent it happening again – that's what wisdom and experience are all about. Put it in perspective. If you miss a bunch of sessions, it's not the end of your exercise life, it's not a total disaster, it's just a blip which you'll even out over the next few days. Exercise lasts for your whole life, so there's plenty of time to make up for it!

get your team around you

Sometimes it's you and only you – like sitting in that pre-event room surrounded by psyched-up competitors – but mostly, you can have a team around you. I can't even start to explain what a difference it makes. Jon is an ex-athlete himself and he did every single training session with me. My family was always there as emotional back-up and for technical support, I had a terrific coach, physiotherapist and dietician. Having a group of people who cared about me and were always on my side was a great inspiration. Even if I really didn't feel like training, I'd make myself do it for them (or because Jon pushed me out the door!).

Who's on your team? Your partner? Family? Friends at work? Tell them your game plan and get excited about it together. Work out any schedule changes together if you'll have to juggle responsibilities. If they want to join in, so much the better.

A word of warning though: don't be surprised if someone tries to throw cold water on your enthusiasm. Humans are basically resistant to change, and less secure individuals may feel threatened by the new, improved you. It's another choice for you to make. Either you can get dragged down by their fear, or you can stick to your guns, confident that a fitter, healthier you will be good for all concerned. Discuss the time requirements and explain you will still be there for them. Suggest they join you now and again. Point out the benefits you'll gain – more energy, less stress, better moods and improved libido (if appropriate!).

enjoy meeting your goals

Here's another good reason to write down your goals and keep a training log: You'll know when you've arrived. The process of achievement has four parts. First, you have to decide what you want to achieve. You have to work for it, then, you have to achieve it. But that's not the end. In order to stay motivated and look forward to achieving your next goal, you deserve a little celebration.

What do you think happens to someone who wins a gold medal? Do you get off the rostrum and go back to work? No way! I had thousands of letters of congratulations, interviews, parties, I was nominated for awards and made to feel incredibly special. The on-going recognition is the true reward for winning, not just the golden gong I keep in a bank vault.

Yet every day, we rush around in our own mini-Olympics, sometimes achieving brilliant things we never thought possible. 'I ran a three mile race!' 'I did 26 press ups!' 'I stuck to my exercise programme for a whole three months!' These things are terrific too, so don't you ever let them slip past unnoticed. My friend Pete Cohen says you should give yourself a little pat on the back whenever you do something right. That's right, a real, physical pat on the back. I know it's difficult to do something so bizarre but go on, try it now. Just reach over your shoulder with one hand, pat pat pat. Does it feel silly? Of course it does! So you get a double bonus – a happy, caring, congratulatory pat with a free giggle! Don't keep them for special occasions, at least one a day is commendable.

deeper than skin

Flick through magazines or TV channels and it seems like 90 per cent of the population is either extremely gorgeous, leggy, fit, slender, successful, or all of the above. Then we look in the mirror and wonder where we fit in. Are we plain? Pretty? Ugly? Normal? One thing's almost certain – we're not much like the people in those magazines. It doesn't do a lot for your confidence, but take heart. Not even the people in the magazines look like that in real life. I've seen myself turn from girl-next-door to amazingly-sexy-glamourpuss in just over an hour. It's astounding what happens when the professionals move in – hairdresser, makeup artist, someone to match your body shape to sumptuous designer clothes, a photographer who does wonderful things with lighting and lenses. After the shoot, changes can be made when the film is developed and again when it's on the designer's screen – it's scary how they can revolutionize someone's looks with a few clever clicks.

So if you enjoy glamorous magazines, fine, just don't confuse them with reality! And if you feel inadequate or depressed after looking at them, just stop. Give them up. Choose to do something cheerful with your spare time instead. Read a novel, dip into a positive thinking book, phone a friend, organize your holiday snaps, go to the cinema, play Scrabble, read a realistic magazine about health and fitness. Or, yes, do some exercise. A good workout is a guaranteed way to appreciate what your body can do, rather than getting

I have to admit, I've never been particularly happy with my body. Especially now, when I'm not as toned as I was, I get cross with my stomach and wish my torso wasn't so short. I'm my number one critic but I know that to be your personal best, you have to rise above it and look with confidence on your strengths instead.

bogged down in details like whether your eyebrows are too bushy. Run up a hill and a pair of frumpy pins are transformed into super-powered pistons. Try a kick boxing class and who cares about chicken wings under the arms – they punch as well as Rocky's.

Confidence in your own abilities shines out of your eyes and gives you more beauty than an expensive face cream ever could. If you can laugh and smile with friends, you'll always be appreciated.

All the same, confidence comes more easily if you know you look your best. Before a race, I had a pamper ritual of shower and hair wash, checked my nails and did my hair. If you look as though you care about yourself, other people give you respect too.

When I raced in different countries with my team-mates, there wasn't always much to do, so us girls would spend hours sitting in hotel rooms, playing with a stack of potions and lotions. Now, with a little boy and a business to run, the face mask is out and quick, simple solutions are in. I use a facial wash, toner and moisturizer every day and if I go out, put on mascara, lipstick and brush my hair (though I still have days when a cap is an easier option).

Overall though, I try to feel confident of my abilities and tell myself people just have to take me for how I look. Experience (and hundreds of letters) has taught me that most people like us the way we are anyway.

body positive

When you take on a new exercise regimen, you considerably deepen your relationship with your body. Even if you begin because you're frustrated with your thighs or sick of your saddlebags, over time it should help you reach a more friendly understanding.

Extending your physical capabilities is a wonderful confidence boost, while weight loss and improved strength follow automatically. But if, like many women, you struggle to appreciate your particular body, here's some techniques which might help smooth the way.

◆ Get naked. Most of us look in the mirror and judge ourselves severely. Our eyes go straight for the bit we like least, we prod it and twist it to measure just how bad it is and say, 'If only my nose/hips/stomach weren't so big.'

Maybe it's time to look again, but with clear, objective eyes. Don't freak out but I'm going to suggest you find a private moment, strip off and stand in front of a full length mirror. Relax, so your body is in its natural state. Look at yourself carefully, as though you were seeing yourself for the first time. Observe how it looks from all sides.

So how do you feel? Vulnerable? Sad? Angry? Happy? Spend some time describing – but not judging – parts of your body which have suffered from bad feelings in the past. Say, 'My thighs are smooth and strong,' rather than, 'My thighs are massive and wobbly.' Your imagination has the power to make things 10 times worse than they really are. Reality may help to neutralize your bad feelings so you can wipe the slate clean and start again.

◆ Meditate. With just five or 10 minutes a day, you can learn to accept and appreciate all aspects of yourself. It gives you a sense of control and lets you know you're worth looking after.

Find a peaceful moment, either first thing in the morning, before you go to bed or around dusk. Sit in an upright chair with your eyes closed. Think about nothing; listen to your breath or feel your heart beating. Thoughts will drop by but try to let them go so your mind is quiet and still. If it helps, explore an image of a beautiful flower, garden or ocean. Stretch out your arms and imagine sending love down your arms and out through your fingertips to someone or something you really love. When you can feel that energy, put your hands on your heart and send the love to yourself, too.

Making a conscious push out of your familiar comfort zone can be fantastic for mind and body. If you tell someone you've abseiled down a cliff face or sailed the high seas, they see beyond the body in front of them and look respectfully at the adventurous soul inside. Don't be afraid of trying new things in front of other people either. It can be hard, but even if you're not very good, you'll be appreciated for having the guts to have a go and it won't be long before your spirit becomes your defining characteristic. Wouldn't it be great to be known as 'the woman with attitude' rather than 'the lady in the blue dress'?

do wacky

As time goes on, life inevitably becomes more straight-laced and serious. It becomes unacceptable to do things which were normal when you were a teenager. Of course we'd be in trouble if we refused to live by any rules at all, but sometimes it's great to let them go. Just for a moment, be an irresponsible, wild, unruly child again. (If you've got kids, you've got a great excuse to do this, though they'll probably hate you for embarrassing them in public.) Visit the beach and run down sandhills while screaming at the top of your lungs. Go on a countryside walk after it's been raining and splash mud all over your clothes (it washes out, I promise). Have a pillow fight with your partner, just like they do on advertisements (it's a fantastic workout too). Or do something you just don't do — go to the opera, eat jellied eels, go to an all-night rave. Or rediscover something you used to enjoy — throw a dinner party, have a camping holiday, dust off the water-colours. Or, take up something completely new you've always hankered after, like sub-aqua diving, pottery or parachuting.

The rules of life are there for a reason but don't let them oppress you. Break them from time to time, and stay in touch with who you are deep down inside.

talk yourself up

Now you're taking brave, proactive steps to improve your lifestyle, you deserve the admiration of everyone else! Every time you talk about it out loud, it's another affirmation for you. People will remember to ask how it's going and give you encouraging vibes when they hear of your success.

People who respect themselves quickly earn the respect of others.

Your new exercise programme is a useful tool for parties or small talk. It's another dimension to your life which may be more appropriate (or interesting!) than the usual topics, such as where you work or live. Showing that you take care of yourself also suggests to listeners you're special enough to be worth the effort. People who respect themselves quickly earn the respect of others. Use this to its best advantage by talking of your exercise only in a positive way. Don't tell them your thighs still chaff when you run or that you're not really any good yet! Concentrate on some of your achievements ('Running for a bus is easy now, whereas it used to make my legs weak all day!') or your goals ('I've entered for a three mile run, which I'm really looking forward to').

think yourself higher

No matter what happens to you over the next eight weeks, promise to do one thing. If you miss sessions, binge on biscuits, decide exercise just isn't your bag, whatever, just do this: give yourself a break. Talk to yourself kindly. Try not to say one mean thing about your body, either out loud or to yourself. Take a tiny piece of time to appreciate the senses of your body. Enjoy a warm bath, absorb the vibrant colours of the outdoors, hear the birds, treat your skin to aromatic lotions and enjoy the sensation of skin on skin. Give up torturing yourself over what you're not; what you are is amazing.

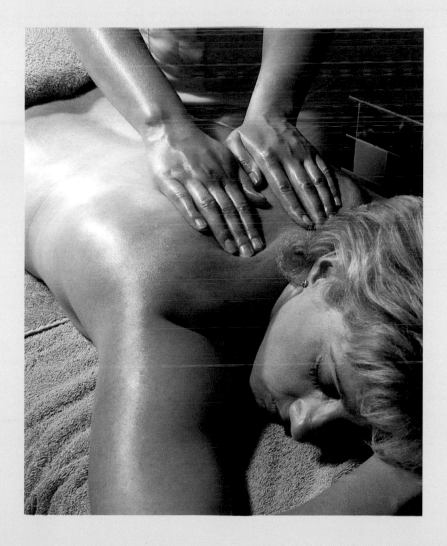

get

physical

At last – you're ready for the fun part! Or is this the part you've been dreading?

'I like thinking about changing my lifestyle – I've done it for months! But now I'm really going to start the exercises it's suddenly got scary. It gives me a funny feeling in my stomach.' (Alison)

It's understandable, especially if you're new to exercise or you've tried before without much luck. Let me reassure you.

If you thought exercise meant ...

◆ no pain, no gain

◆ running three times around the playing field

◆ leotards with thong bottoms

◆ huge, bulgy muscles

◆ complicated routines

◆ repetitive movements in a gym

◆ being made to look silly

... forget it! That's old fashioned, out of date and certainly not to be found in these pages. To me, fitness is a way to get more out of life.

In just eight weeks, you can:

◆   increase your energy

◆   improve your sleep patterns

◆   find new confidence and a sense of achievement

◆   feel calmer

◆   have a sense of control over your body

◆   feel good about how you look

◆   have firmer muscle tone

◆   fit your clothes better

◆   discover a sport you love

◆   have more activities to choose from at the weekend

◆   develop a totally new dream or ambition

◆   start habits which will increase your life span

◆   give yourself the tools to enjoy life at every age.

I don't expect you to become a slave to exercise, working out twice a day, six days a week. You'd be mad to do that (or training for the Olympics). Rather, the idea is to integrate exercise into your normal life. To fit it in with the least fuss and inconvenience. To use it as a tool to make your life more enjoyable and manageable.

It's all about options. My exercise programme includes a range of options, so you can choose whatever fits with your lifestyle. Choose a session you can do at the gym one day; work out at home another day. Choose a jog on Tuesday; play tennis with friends on Saturday. The only rule is, whatever you choose, you have to enjoy it.

three parts to a fitter you

1. RESISTANCE TRAINING

Also known as weights or weight training, resistance work used to be considered bloke's stuff. Not any more. It's a vital component for women, not just for sleek, toned muscles but because of its amazing anti-ageing properties.

◆ It helps maintain bone strength.

Did you know that bones live and change? Just like muscle, they grow stronger in response to 'weight-bearing exercise' – anything which demands they cope with a heavier load than normal. Running and weight lifting count; swimming and cycling, where the body weight is supported, do not.

Ultimately, weak bones lead to osteoporosis, one of the biggest causes of premature ageing, disability, or death (one in five hip fractures results in death). You may associate this disease with frail old ladies, but the problems can start any time after the age of about 25. Disused bones lose density, becoming porous and weak.

The most fragile points of the body are hips, spine and wrist. While the spine and hips benefit from exercise such as jogging or skipping, where your feet leave the ground, you can strengthen all three points with dumbbells or a simple resistance band. Great news if you're creaky at the knees.

◆ It helps maintain muscle mass.

Does that fail to excite you? Turn it around and it becomes a hot favourite with just about everyone: resistance training helps reduce body fat. Seriously! Most of us assume that aerobic work, like running, cycling and swimming, are best for weight loss because you burn so many calories while you do them. But have you ever looked at a calorie counter on a machine at the gym?

get physical

After a hard, sweaty 20 minute cycle, you might find you've burned a measly 150 calories. About the same as two rice cakes. And your raised metabolism keeps burning them for only about 15 minutes after you've finished.

While this is helpful, training with weights can change the way your body functions all day, every day – that's when the real body-shaping begins.

Let me tell you something which will blow your socks off. One pound of body fat burns just two calories a day, while one pound of muscle burns 35. That's right – 35 lovely calories, just for sitting around doing nothing! Muscle simply takes more effort to maintain, so the more muscle you have, the more fat you'll burn, whether you're working out or fast asleep.

After the age of 35, we start losing muscle at the rate of half a pound a year. Between the ages of 25 and 64, we typically lose 30 to 40 per cent of muscle mass. That's why

muscle is important for health as well as body shape,

and resistance work is by far the best way to do it.

What's more, if you build a good base of muscle, your body will look better, regardless of body fat. It's this tone and definition which gives you shape and makes you feel in charge. Plus, if you want to be practical, improved strength makes daily life that little bit easier. Children, groceries, filing cabinets ... whatever needs to be lifted or moved, you'll be able to do it more easily and safely.

Just one note about the effects of resistance training: it's all about body fat loss, not weight loss. Muscle weighs more than fat, so although you'll look slimmer and feel tonnes better, you may not see any difference on the scales. Forget about them – find other ways to measure your improvements, such as how well your clothes fit, how vital you feel or how firm your arms are when you give them a prod.

2. AEROBIC CONDITIONING

'Aerobic' means 'with air', so this is any type of work which makes you breathe harder than normal. It includes brisk walking, running, cycling, swimming, housework, tennis, skiing, dancing, skating, Step aerobics, football... it's all the things you imagine yourself enjoying when you think about an energetic, active you. It's great for emotional and physical wellbeing.

◆ **It improves your cardiovascular system: your heart, lungs, and the processes they go through to deliver oxygen to your blood, and blood to your muscles.**

As you improve aerobically, the muscle fibres surrounding your heart become thicker and stronger, so more blood is pumped with each stroke. Your blood circulation becomes more efficient, so your heart rate is slower at rest. At my peak fitness, my resting heart-rate was 48 beats per minute. (Now it's gone up to 64 beats per minute.) What's the benefit of a slower heart rate? Think of it as a scale: your heart only has the capacity to work so hard at any particular age. (As a rough guide, it's 220, minus your age. So if you're 40 years old, your heart can only possibly thump at 180 beats a minute, no matter how fast you run.) If your heart beats at level 7 out of 10 while you read a book, it will hammer frighteningly loud, at level 9, if you just climb a flight of stairs. If it normally beats at level 3, you have far more capacity to be active and could run a half marathon without hitting level 8.

◆ **It links into your fat-burning system.**

Aerobic exercise is famed for its fat-burning properties. This stems from research which showed it was the only type of exercise to burn fat as well as glucose. (Glucose is a sugar we get from

carbohydrates like bread and pasta. It's quick-release energy, whereas fat is more difficult to convert, so is only used as a last resort.) While this sounds terrific, two factors make it more complicated: your fat-burning system only kicks in after 20 minutes, and, it works best when you exercise as a moderate intensity. This was a revelation, but it brought problems too. Suddenly, everyone was exercising half as hard as they used to, so although they burned a higher proportion of fat, the total number of calories was far less than if they worked out at a higher aerobic intensity. If you want to burn more fat, you really need to burn as many calories as you can.

So where does this leave you? To make the most of your fat-burning system, try to include one or two aerobic workouts a week which last at least half an hour. As your fitness increases, so should the length of these workouts. Remember it doesn't have to be flat out – go for a cycle ride with friends at the weekend and a couple of hours can whiz by before you know it.

To significantly improve your cardiovascular system and chew through large numbers of calories, you could include one shorter, harder aerobic session a week. Try interval training, where you alternate an intense burst of exercise with a slow, recovery burst. For example, jog for two minutes, then run hard for one minute. Repeat several times.

There are additional benefits to aerobic workouts. For one, the longer, slow sessions help your body become efficient at using fat for fuel. Two, aerobic fitness helps you feel more confident during daily activities, such as running for a bus, walking quickly or playing with your kids. And three, this is one type of fitness which is really just an excuse for fun. Think of all the walking, biking, inline skating or tennis you can enjoy in the name of aerobic capacity.

3. FLEXIBILITY

Most of us want to lose body fat, tone muscles, get fit and look fabulous. Writhing around on the floor doing stretches just doesn't have the same appeal. No wonder flexibility is the most neglected part of fitness but believe me, it's important.

◆ **It protects your muscles against injury.**

Whether you do a sport like football which makes you dart around in all directions, or a steady activity like jogging, your muscles must be prepared for any position you demand of them. Stretching imitates the moves in a smooth and controlled manner. It takes the muscles beyond what you'd normally do, so you have a safer range of motion when you do your activity for real. Explosive moves like hurdling throws your body into weird positions. If my muscles hadn't been used to it, something would have torn or pulled long before I made it to the Olympics.

get physical

67

Take some time to stretch out — your body will thank you.

◆ It balances your body.

Regular stretching can relieve tension, correct imbalances in your posture and ease pain from intense exercise. It's also good if you suffer from low-back pain, which can stem from tightness in the hamstrings or muscles around the hips and pelvis.

◆ It adds elegance.

If you want an aesthetic reason for stretching, it keeps the muscles long and lean. Do too much strength work without stretching and the muscles become bulky and compact – probably not the look you're after.

If I get out of bed in the morning feeling stiff and creaky, it's because I've skimped on my stretches. Flexibility becomes even more important with age. If your body is able to move more freely, it is more able to right itself if you lose your balance, and avoid muscle damage if you do take a tumble.

After stretching, the muscles only stay elongated for a few hours, so ideally, you should build a stretch session into your daily routine. Luckily, it doesn't have to be very long – I used to do 45 minutes a day, but just 10 minutes is enough for normal life.

You must make sure your muscles are 'warm' before you stretch them, not just temperature-wise but that they've been moving for at least five minutes so the blood pumping through them makes them pliable. That's why it's ideal to add 10 minutes of stretching onto the end of your workout. The muscles have worked hard, they're fully receptive to a good stretch, and it will help remove waste product from the muscles which could cause soreness the next day.

However, if you have to rush off after your gym session, you can stretch later on. I find it a nice, sociable activity you can do while chatting with friends or in front of the TV. Just take five minutes to warm up, say walk around the block, climb up and down the stairs or vacuum the carpet before you collapse onto the floor and start your routine.

Always listen to your body. Stretch deep enough so you can feel it without hurting yourself and work within your own limits – some people are naturally more flexible than others, so don't try to copy them. After your first stretch, take a breath, exhale and try to push a tiny bit further. Hold each stretch for 20–30 seconds in total. Just one stretch is enough for each muscle group.

get physical

questions, questions...

HOW OFTEN SHOULD I WORK OUT?

I expect you'd like me to give you a straight answer: you must do three sessions a week, each lasting no less than 53 minutes plus 4 minutes of stretching and 98 press ups. But it's not going to work like that. This programme is all about taking responsibility for yourself, so I want you to decide what your goals are, and then decide if – realistically – you can commit the time needed to achieve them.

Here's what it takes to achieve some basic goals (assuming your diet stays the same):

◆ **To maintain current fitness: 1 hour a week**

◆ **To improve health and fitness: 2–3 hours a week**

◆ **To significantly improve health, fitness and change body shape in eight weeks: 3–4 hours a week.**

Okay, hands up who's thinking, 'Three hours! Where am I going to find three hours when I don't have four seconds to brush my hair!' Don't panic! Remember:

◆ **There's 24 hours in a day, 168 in a week.**

◆ **Your workout hours don't have to be consecutive – it counts just the same whether you schedule 40 minutes, three days a week; two hour-long slots during the week, one hour at the weekend or three 10 minute slots, six days a week.**

◆ **This is time invested, never time wasted. Don't you think the benefits above are worth a little time?**

I suggest you initially aim for three hours a week, broken up any way which fits your schedule, but adding up to:

♦ **Two full resistance workouts (using either bands or dumbbells at home, or dumbbells in the gym). Total time = one hour, 30 minutes.**

♦ **Two aerobic workouts, intense enough to make you hot and sweaty. Total time = one hour.**

♦ **One enjoyable activity, intense enough to make you slightly out of breath, once a week or week-end. Total time = 30 minutes upwards.**

After the first few weeks, you may find time and inclination to slot in even more activity – great! If you can stretch any of the three sections so you total four hours a week, you'll make great strides.

As well as the official workouts, make a resolution to do something small, every day. Just move your body, to keep things ticking over. Walk up stairs and escalators, walk to the shops at lunchtime, dance to a song on the radio ... it will help your body get used to moving and give you an energizing burst.

HOW LONG SHOULD I WORK OUT FOR?

None of the sessions in this programme should take you longer than 45 minutes. That means, including a quick change and shower, you should be done within the hour. If you're pushed for time, break it down into smaller sections – you could do the upper body weights before breakfast, the lower body when you get home from work and the abdominal exercises before bed. Or, you could cycle to the shops for fifteen minutes in the morning and take a fifteen minute jog in the evening. Or, you could arrange a family hike at the weekend and be out for two hours, so don't limit yourself! It's all great exercise and it all helps towards your goals.

CAN I SKIP THE WARM-UP AND COOL-DOWN IF I'M BUSY?

An exercise programme should be for life, not just eight weeks, so it's important to take care of your body. Doctors, coaches, physiotherapists and personal trainers all recommend you do a warm-up before you start working hard: five minutes of easy exercise to warm the muscles and get the blood flowing.

If you're pushed for time, maybe you can incorporate the warm-up into your preparation? Like it or not, I always seem to spend five minutes running after Finley before I go out for my morning run, which counts as a warm-up. Maybe you can bike to the gym? Walk briskly to the swimming pool? Vacuum the floor before you get out your resistance bands? It doesn't matter what you do, but a few minutes to prepare your muscles for work significantly decreases your chances of muscle strain or injury. If I wasn't preoccupied with potties and Thomas the Tank Engine, I would use the time time mentally prepare for my workout – it's good to calm down and focus on what you're about to achieve.

A cool-down is much the same, except at the end of your workout. If you've just finished a testing aerobic session, take the last few minutes to wind down, get your breath back and congratulate yourself for working so hard. If you stop suddenly, your muscles can seize up, becoming tight and uncomfortable. Make the most of their warm and receptive state by doing some stretches.

WHAT IF I'M STARTING FROM SCRATCH?

If you're basically healthy, you should be safe to start this exercise programme even if you're older, overweight, or have been inactive for a long time. However, you should check with your doctor if you have any of the following:

The warm-up is as important as the work-out.

- ◆ chest pains, high blood pressure or heart disease

- ◆ chest trouble, like asthma or bronchitis

- ◆ serious back problems or a slipped disc

- ◆ trouble with joint pain or arthritis

- ◆ diabetes

- ◆ recently had an illness or operation

- ◆ doubts about your ability to exercise.

Exercise can help all of these conditions, but you should talk it over with your doctor first.

Build up gradually. If you work too hard one day, you'll feel too sore and exhausted to continue the next, so always work within your limits.

I FEEL BREATHLESS WHEN I JOG OR CYCLE FAST – SURELY THIS CAN'T BE GOOD FOR ME?

If you're used to a sedentary lifestyle, the effects of exercise can be a shock. Rest assured, breathlessness is perfectly normal. In fact, it's one way to tell if you're working hard enough for your exercise to be effective – if you're slightly out of breath, you know your heart rate has increased, your blood is pumping faster, you're burning more calories and on the way to improvement.

DOESN'T IT HAVE TO HURT TO DO ANY GOOD?

To make physical improvements, you have to push yourself continually. Your muscles only get stronger, your lungs only bigger, if you give them a slightly harder challenge every week.

At first, these challenges might seem to produce 'pain', but once you know your body better, you'll know the difference between 'good pain' and 'bad pain'. Good pain is a signal which tells you yes, you're working hard, yes, you're pushing yourself and yes, you'll be a little bit fitter tomorrow. Good pain doesn't really hurt at all – it can actually be part of the enjoyment of exercise, and it goes away as soon as the exertion is over.

'Bad pain' is not good at all, and if you ever feel it, I recommend you stop straight away. This is an intense feeling when you know something's not working properly. It probably remains painful after you stop what you're doing. Get an ice pack onto it if appropriate and if it doesn't improve, seek medical attention.

WHAT DO I WEAR?

Whatever suits your body shape, location, mood and exercise. Leotards have long gone – shorts, t-shirts and loose trousers are the most common choice. I like to wear tight leggings or shorts because my legs get too hot in jogging bottoms, plus a baggy t-shirt if it's cool outside or a vest top if it's warm.

If you'd like to celebrate your commitment to fitness by splashing out on a new outfit, technical fabrics make a big difference to comfort. Look for a fabric which is designed to take moisture away from the skin and keep you dry (a process called 'wicking'). Many brands have their own trade names for this type of fabric but they do a similar job.

For women, the one item I'd recommend you buy is a sports bra, especially if you do high impact sports like running, tennis or aerobics. There's a small amount of research to suggest this type of exercise makes your boobs sag – I'm more worried about comfort and confidence. Nothing feels worse than bouncing around uncontrollably in public, so a good bra which either compresses or cups the breasts in place, is money well spent.

For everyone, the other must is footwear. Every time your foot lands during running or jumping, it sends shock waves through your body of four to eight times your body weight. That's why it's essential to wear supportive trainers, even if you don't yet see yourself as a 'serious' exerciser

Cross trainers are sometimes seen as a 'jack of all trades, master of none' but they are a good option if you do small amounts of many different activities, such as resistance work, a half hour run and an aerobics class a week.

If you find you enjoy one particular activity and tally up more than one or two hours a week, sport specific shoes will increase your comfort and protect your joints.

Runners, for example, will be overjoyed by their first pair of running shoes – the lighter weight makes you fly! They don't have to be super-expensive but you should go to a proper running shop, where you'll receive good advice from a knowledgeable sales person. There are several running styles and it's important to find a pair of shoes which match your particular gait.

Sports like tennis, football or squash have completely different demands on your feet, so again, it's well worth buying appropriate shoes.

With the correct support and protection, you'll play your sport better, feel more stable and confident, and your shoes will last longer too.

Why not treat yourself to a new pair of trainers.

WHAT IF I JUST WANT TO LOSE FAT FROM MY HIPS AND THIGHS?

Wouldn't it be great if you could choose which bit of fat to burn next? Many women try to get a flat stomach by doing zillions of crunches. That's called 'spot reduction' and sadly, it doesn't work. When we burn fat, it comes from all over the body, though the newest bits of fat are usually the first to go. That means problem areas like hips and thighs are often the last to change; women's bodies are genetically programmed to hang onto them as long as possible.

Exercises like squats, lunges, hill walking and stair climbing are good for hips and thighs but not because they burn fat in those areas. It just so happens that the buttock and thigh muscles are among the largest in the body, so working them hard burns more calories than you would with a small movement like a tricep dip. Plus, firming up the muscle gives a nice shape to the area and helps to make it pert and firm.

I'VE NEVER USED RESISTANCE BEFORE – I WON'T BULK UP, WILL I?

Out of all the men you know who exercise, how many end up with a chest like two ripe melons? Not many, I'll bet, even though they're full of testosterone, the hormone which controls muscle growth. Women have only a tenth the amount of testosterone and almost all of us would find it hard to build large muscles without intensive training and very heavy weights.

Through using resistance bands or dumbbells in this programme, you'll strengthen, tone and define, but you won't bulk up.

CAN I WATCH TV OR READ WHILE I WORK OUT?

Theoretically, yes, but for the next eight weeks I'm going to say no. Why? Because I really want this programme to work for you.

To maximize the rewards from all the time and energy you're committing to your body and fitness, you really need to think about what you're doing.

Look at any line-up of athletes before a race. There's not too much to do while you wait for the gun to go off but they don't stand there, idly dreaming about their favourite soap. Their faces are a picture of concentration. They think about what they're doing, why they're doing it and how they're going to make their dreams come true. They want to achieve their personal best and so do you – that's why I'd like you to follow their lead.

When you work out, think about what you do. As you do resistance training, imagine the muscle you're working and feel it through the movement. Gauge how hard it's working. Has it done its dash after 12 repetitions or could you squeeze out a little more? When you do aerobic work, think about your technique. Could you be more streamlined? Is your posture correct? Are you breathing hard enough to make a difference?

Exercising your body is a really interesting process. I'm sure after the first week or two you'll find it easy to concentrate on what you're doing without distraction. If, after eight weeks, you simply hate it so much that you can't possibly do it without switching on *Friends*, then sure, you're better to do that than not work out at all, but give it a good shot first.

SHOULD I JOIN A GYM?

Not everyone has the time, money or inclination to join a gym. If this is your last barrier to getting fit, forget it! With my home-based programme you can do exactly the same exercises in your front room, using simple pieces of equipment like resistance bands or small dumbbells.

The hardest part about working out at home is the proximity of the sofa, the kitchen, the bedroom which needs tidying and all the other little chores you'd usually ignore. When you have an exercise session to do, they can suddenly become incredibly interesting! Be firm with yourself; plan your exercise time and give it the value it

*Should I join
a gym?*

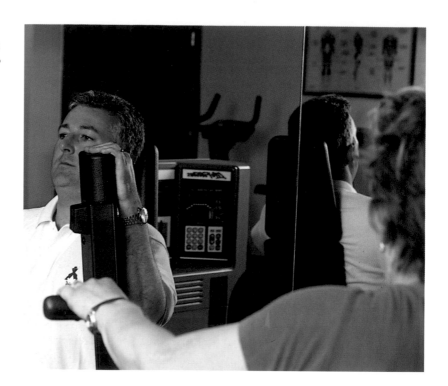

deserves. Your training log will help to remind you what you have
to achieve and you'll get that warm feeling when you tick it off.

If you're interested in joining a gym, look for the one closest to
your home or work. If you have to make a special trip, you're less
likely to visit – just getting there is another mental barrier. Once
you find a gym which fits your schedule, it can become a
satisfying place to hang out. You arrive, you know exactly what
you have to do, you get the job done and then get on with your
day. Most gyms offer variety, which is good for motivation –
classes like group cycling, circuit training or yoga can broaden
your choice of strength or aerobic activities. Plus many gyms offer
saunas and steam rooms for unwinding, and bars or cafes for post-
workout socializing (just watch out for chips and beer).

If you're on a budget, many city councils have improved their
gym facilities in recent years and provide very good set-ups at a
reasonable price.

Even if you fall in love with your gym, don't forget to take your
workout outside now and then. Fresh air and sunlight are
excellent for mind as well as body!

About 60 per cent of us suffer from back pain at some time during our lives. It's the third most commonly reported bodily symptom after headache and tiredness. You're right to be concerned about looking after your back, but you'd be wrong to molly-coddle it.

Studies have shown the best remedy for low back pain is exercise such as walking, cycling and swimming.

It's also a sure-fire prevention method. Injuries often occur because the muscles surrounding the spine are too weak to support it. If you strengthen the trunk area, your muscles will do the work instead of your spine, saving it from overload.

'Core stability', as it's known, is fundamental to exercise methods such as yoga and Pilates, and can be improved during your resistance sessions. It doesn't mean hundreds of stomach crunches. If you think about the girdle of muscles around your stomach and back while you do bicep curls, bench press, squats – in fact, any resistance exercise – and use them to hold your trunk steady, you'll improve core stability as well.

Whenever you exercise, try to keep your spine in 'neutral' (see p88). That simply means the most natural position for your back. Holding this comfortable, tall position while you work out is great for your back. As the core muscles strengthen, they will help your posture and endurance. You'll be able to stay upright and powerful to the very end of a long aerobic session, which will in turn keep the air flowing easily to your lungs.

By the way, if you've ever wondered about weights belts, don't. Those wide, leather contraptions were popular a few decades ago but new research proves they're worse than useless. Bulked-up blokes used them to hold their spine stable while they threw massive weights around. In fact they prevented them using their own stabilizers – if they tried to lift the same weights without the belt, they'd fold up like a flower. Not very sensible.

get physical

I'VE TRIED EXERCISE BUT IT DIDN'T WORK –
WHAT DID I DO WRONG?

Everyone is unique but human physiology stays constant. Almost everybody in the world (except for a tiny minority with a severe medical problem) functions to the same metabolic formula: calories in versus calories out. If you take in more calories than you burn off, the extra energy is stored as fat. If you use more than you consume, you lose weight.

If you honestly follow this programme and eat nutritious food only when you're hungry, you can't help but improve your mental and physical state.

By honestly, I mean you do all the sessions as described and you put in the effort to do every exercise properly. Listen to your muscles; if they're not really working, increase the resistance or the repetitions, do them more slowly, enjoy the sweat and 'good pain'.

The other, most common reason an exercise programme fails has nothing to do with your body. It's your mind – your motivation and commitment run out of steam. Don't let it happen! Give this programme your best shot for eight weeks, pat yourself on the back, set some new goals and get back into it.

HOW LONG BEFORE I SEE THE DIFFERENCE?

If you honestly follow this exercise programme and learn to eat more healthily, you should feel a difference within two weeks. I'm not promising a 'two-weeks-to-a-new-you' miracle, that's not humanly possible (not on a long-term basis, anyway). But after just two weeks, you'll start to notice some of the differences outlined at the start of this chapter. Stick at it and they'll keep on coming; by week eight your goals will be within reach.

Alison

- ◆ active job
- ◆ new weight gain
- ◆ unpredictable schedule
- ◆ wants to tone up

Because her job is very physical, Alison assumed it would keep her fit as well. She probably is, compared to an office worker, but the body quickly adapts to whatever you throw at it. Alison has done the same job for 11 years and ridden horses since she was 5, so her body isn't challenged by the work she does.

Now she's past the age of 25, her body is officially ageing – scary, isn't it! That's why the handles are starting to appear. They're still very new though, so it won't take long to regain control. The key is to give her body enough physical challenge. She must use a high enough level of resistance to tire the muscles after each workout and really tune in to how hard she works.

Alison's other difficulty is her schedule – early mornings, late nights and being away from home can make it difficult to fit in exercise. She needs to develop a selection of activities (and gym bags) she can fit to her circumstances. The resistance bands can be slung in a bag and used in a small room, and for aerobic work, I would suggest running. It's the ideal transportable sport, especially pleasant for Alison as she's lucky enough to be in the countryside a lot. Running also demands its own type of fitness so although she has a good fitness base, she will feel the effects in her heart and lungs straight away. Maybe it will also inspire her to cut down on cigarettes.

Alternatively, I've heard about a pair of inline skates which she bought and never used. Skating is great for the aerobic system and lower body muscles, so it could be worth digging them out.

Lucy

- ◆ runs and walks regularly
- ◆ wants to avoid bulking up
- ◆ wants to flatten stomach, define muscles and slim legs

Lucy does well to fit as much exercise into her busy life as she already does. Her regular walks with the dogs are enough to impress many people and gives her a good aerobic fitness base.

The one thing which could make a real difference is resistance training. This will give her the muscle tone she wants while helping to speed up fat loss. She can whip through the programme in half an hour or 45 minutes, breaking it into two if need be. Lunchtime is a possible slot on the days she works from home; some exercises could even be knocked out when she walks the dogs early in the morning. Surely no-one would be around at that time to see a mad woman doing press-ups in the park?

As she's one of the few women who tend to build muscle easily, stretching is very important. This will help to make the muscles long and elegant, rather than short and chunky. This goes for stomach muscles too – a million sit-ups a day won't help if the muscles aren't stretched. You'll end up with a muscular spare-tyre instead of flat abs.

To push herself in the aerobic department, Lucy could build in interval training to her weekly run. A burst of fast running followed by a burst of normal or slow running, say a minute or two minutes of each, would fit a lot more challenge into the same amount of time and make life more interesting.

Karen

- body never the same after children
- low energy
- tried exercise in the past but given up
- wants to slim the middle area

During pregnancy, the lower abdominals stretch ... and stretch ... and stretch. The muscles which used to hold internal organs like a natural corset lose their strength and elasticity. During caesarean, as Karen has experienced, the muscles are surgically separated, making them weaker than ever. Many women also increase the fat deposits around their hips and thighs. This is hormonal, but it can be difficult to get rid of after birth especially if, as Karen admits, being pregnant meant open season on the food front.

With Karen, some of the problem comes from lack of motivation and self-consciousness. She should do the resistance exercises in the privacy of her own home and for aerobic work, could try swimming, aqua aerobics or cycling, which are less 'public' than running. After the first few weeks – once the changes start coming – she might feel comfortable enough to start running again.

To improve motivation, Karen needs to be incredibly strict about keeping her training log. She must remember every day why she's working out and remind herself about the positive effects it's having on her energy and confidence.

As she's such a sociable person, it might help to link up with a 'fitness buddy'. Even if they don't always exercise together, it might help to have a friend she can compare notes or tips with, or if they go for a goal together.

Her children are just about old enough to enjoy outdoor life themselves. Family walks or cycles at the weekend could count for a good aerobics session.

Neil

◆ busy desk job
◆ travels two days a week
◆ growing stomach
◆ wants to regain fitness and lose body fat

Neil knows exactly what to do – go to the gym three lunch times a week, just as he did when training for the marathon. So why doesn't he do it? In his demanding job, he's given fitness a lower priority than churning through another hour of work.

His problem is pure commitment: once he gives working out a higher ranking in his mind, he'll be motivated enough to achieve anything.

He currently uses weights machines on the rare occasions he makes it into the gym. He should learn to use free weights – dumbbells and barbells – instead. They demand more from both brain and body. He'll really have to think about what he's doing, which makes the workout more interesting and profitable. Plus, because he has to control the movement himself, using free weights would engage the core muscles around the trunk. This will help to strengthen Neil's wobbly tum while providing a more thorough workout.

As he works out within a tight time frame, he should make sure his aerobic bursts are as intense as possible. Like Lucy, he should do interval training on the treadmill and elliptical trainer. After a five minute warm-up, I want him to fight for a real sweat!

Pam

- ◆ gained weight during menopause
- ◆ enjoys activity and plays tennis
- ◆ wants to lose weight around stomach and backside

Those hormones go wild during menopause and apart from drugs, there's very little which can control them – not even exercise! While weight gain is one common symptom, two more important ones are less obvious: a dramatic rise in the risk of both heart disease and osteoporosis. At least exercise can help here.

As muscle mass decreases with maturity, it's easy to see how body fat levels creep up regardless of hormones, although Pam's given herself a head start by enjoying exercise off-and-on throughout her life. She's never tried resistance training though, so this is the perfect time to activate that gym membership. With a three-day working week, it shouldn't be hard to fit in at least one visit for a weights session, and maybe another for a swim or a class.

Pam shouldn't be scared of 'heavy' weights – despite her maturity, she still has to work her muscles until they feel fatigued before she'll see any improvement.

Tennis is a good aerobic workout although singles is more effective than doubles. It's also weight-bearing exercise (she has to carry her body weight around the court) which is good for maintaining bone density. Another solid aerobic session would be helpful – that bicycle might be a good start! Power walking is a 'safe' option for older people but running would be better. Many women take up running after the age of 50 and quickly build excellent stamina. With a solid fitness base like Pam's, a marathon in a year's time wouldn't be out of the question!

the
exercises

workout jargon

I'm not impressed by fancy words but a few terms are helpful to know. These are used in the fitness world by everyone, not just top athletes, so you're likely to hear them often.

Repetitions/reps
When you lift a weight, then lower it back to the start position, that's a repetition. It's the completion of a single movement. I recommend 8–12 repetitions for each resistance exercise.

Sets
A group of repetitions. In the past, the most common resistance programme was three sets of 8–12 repetitions. I recommend you only do one set, because recent research shows the gains you get from two extra sets is relatively small. If you want to get serious muscles, go ahead and do three sets. If time, all-round fitness and toning are more important, stick to one.

Muscle fatigue
The point at which a muscle cannot do another repetition, also known as muscle failure. It sounds frightening, but don't worry, it's normal! You will recover in 30 seconds or so, though you may feel slightly feeble for a couple of hours. It's part of the body's natural strengthening system. When you rest, the muscles will mend themselves and grow back stronger – that's why you must reach fatigue for the best improvements.

Neutral spine
Your back's most natural position. To find neutral spine, stand with your legs shoulder-width apart. Rock onto the balls of your feet, then the heels, then find the middle point where your weight is comfortably and evenly distributed. Soften your knees. Gently curl your spine and pelvis inwards, then arch outwards. Repeat a couple of times. Find the half-way point between these two extremes and use your trunk muscles to hold you in place. Lift

your chest slightly, relax your shoulders and lengthen your neck. You should have a slight curve in the lower back – my back has a naturally pronounced curve which works for me but don't copy it exactly! Try to maintain neutral during every exercise you do (and in daily life too!). Support it by pulling your belly towards your spine, to tighten your deepest abdominal muscle.

Locked joints

Elbows and knees work like hinges – they only open so far. If they're accidentally pushed further, the result could be a nasty injury. Keep your elbows and knees 'soft' or very slightly bent during resistance exercise, so when you stand or open your arms, the joints can't 'lock'.

stretches

Here's a selection of stretches covering the main muscle groups used during the resistance workout. Follow the sequence to warm your muscles up before doing any exercise and to prevent injury. The same exercises should be done after your workout or exercise session to prevent aches, pains and stiffening up. Hold each one for 10–20 seconds after your workout.

START:

1 Sit on the floor with your knees bent, soles of your feet together. Don't bring your feet in too close to your body.
2 Make sure you are on your 'sitting bones' and that your pelvis is square.

ACTION:

1 Breathe in to prepare, and sit up tall to lengthen the spine.
2 Pull your tummy button towards your spine. Breathe out as you lift up from your hips and relax your upper body forward. Bring your head towards your ankles, but only as far as comfortable.
3 In this position, take 8 breaths. Relax into the stretch each time. Reach forward but maintain a strong centre. Breathe into your lower rib cage and back.
4 On your last out-breath, straighten up slowly, one vertebra at a time.

TIP

Relax your shoulders.

START:

1 Sit on the floor with one leg out in front of you, the other bent and dropped open. The sole of your bent leg can rest against the other knee.

2 Check your spine is in neutral, your pelvis is square, and that you are sitting on your 'sitting bones'. The straight leg should be in line with your hip.

ACTION:

1 Breathe in to prepare and lengthen up through the spine.

2 Breathe out, pull your tummy button towards your spine and gently stretch forward from the hips.

3 Take 8 breaths in this position, relaxing into the stretch. Breathe into your lower rib cage and back. Keep your weight even on both sitting bones.

4 After your last in-breath, breathe out as you straighten up, one vertebra at a time.

5 Repeat on the other side.

TIP

Keep a slight bend in your extended knee. Put your hands under it if it tends to lock out.

the exercises

START:

1 Stand with your legs slightly wider than shoulder-width apart.
2 Breathe in to prepare and check your back is in neutral.
3 Raise one arm above your head, keeping the elbow soft.

ACTION:

1 Breathe out as you bend to the side, making a long body and reaching out with your extended arm.
2 Hold the stretch, then return to start and repeat on the other side.

START:

1 Stand with your legs hip-width apart, spine in neutral.
2 Raise one arm above your head, then bend it at the elbow so your hand falls between your shoulder blades.

ACTION:

1 Place the other hand on your elbow and gently push down until you feel a comfortable stretch in your upper arm.
2 Straighten both arms above your head and repeat on the other side.

TIP

Take care not to lean forwards or backwards. Imagine you're sandwiched between two panes of glass.

be your best

92

START:

1 Stand with your feet hip-width apart. You may wish to stand in front of a chair or other support.

ACTION:

1 Bend one knee and grasp the top of the foot (the shoelace area) with the hand on the same side.
2 Touch the chair or a wall if you need to stop wobbling or keep your posture.
3 To increase the stretch, tilt your pelvis forward a fraction and pull the foot in towards your buttocks.

START:

1 Stand with one foot a step in front of the other, both feet pointing forwards.

ACTION:

1 Keeping your spine in neutral, sink down until you can feel a stretch in the calf of your back leg. Keep both feet flat on the floor.
2 Stand up, change legs and repeat on the other side.

TIP

Keep your knee pointing downwards, not spreading out to the side.

the exercises

93

dumbbell workout

If you belong to a gym, you can do these exercises with dumbbells in the free weights area. This section is often populated by muscley men waving a 40lb dumbbell in each hand. Don't be put off – you pay your membership too!

Choose a weight which matches the size of the muscle you target. For bigger muscles, like biceps, shoulders or chest, start with 5lb (2 kilos). For smaller muscles like the triceps, go for 2lb or 3lb.

As you improve, keep the challenges coming by using a progressively heavier dumbbell. Remember that you should always feel so fatigued after 8–12 repetitions that squeezing another one out is virtually impossible. If you feel fine after 12 reps, keep going until you tire out, but make a note in your training log to chose a heavier weight next time.

You can do the same exercises at home too, if you decide to invest in a set of dumbbells. You do need a firm, raised platform to work from though. I've used a Step, which can also be used for aerobic work, but a weights bench is more comfortable. They're often available second hand through free ads newspapers (often nearly new – someone else's failure could be your gain). Look for one which is sturdy, adjustable, and can be collapsed flat for storage.

TARGETS: CHEST

You can't exercise for bigger breasts but this gives them a nice platform to stand on! I   e it even more than a barbell bench press, because dumbbells stimulate the chest muscles more and it's easier on your shoulders. It can feel awkward at first but persist – sometimes the clumsy ones are the most challenging.

START:

1 Sit on the end of the bench, a dumbbell in each hand.
2 Rest the dumbbells on your thighs as you roll onto your back, bringing the weights up to your chest.
3 Keep your feet on the floor and maintain the natural curves of your back and neck.
4 Pull your shoulder blades back and lift the weights to an inch above your shoulders, palms facing towards your feet, elbows out.

ACTION:

1 Press the weights straight up, keeping them over your upper chest. Keep your wrists strong, thumbs facing each other. Stop just before your elbows lock.
2 Slowly lower to the start position, feeling a slight stretch in your chest muscles as your elbows drop a fraction below the level of the bench.

the exercises

TIP

Be areful the dumbbells don't sway over your face.

TARGETS: SHOULDERS

A good way to put nice 'caps' on your shoulders – the start of a shapely arm!

START:

1 Sit on a bench with your feet flat on the floor, a dumbbell in each hand.
2 Breathe in to engage your trunk muscles and check your spine is in neutral.
3 Lift the dumbbells so they're several inches out from your shoulders, but at the same level. Stick your elbows out and face your palms forward.

ACTION:

1 Slowly press the dumbbells up and in, so they nearly touch above your head. Stop just before your elbows lock. Don't let the weights wobble back and forth.
2 Lower the dumbbells back to shoulder height. Stop before your elbows can rest on your sides.

TIP

Keep your head and neck in the same, natural position, not leaning back. Look forwards with your chin up, shoulders squared and chest high.

TARGETS: UPPER BACK

Apart from looking making you look great in a strappy dress, these muscles are responsible for an upright posture and open shoulders. Good posture not only cuts down on stress pains, but makes you feel more confident too.

START:

1 Rest your left knee and hand on the bench. Plant your right foot flat on the floor and hold a dumbbell in your right hand, palm facing towards you.
2 Check your torso is parallel with the floor – it should stay like this throughout the movement. Keep your neck in line with your spine, face towards the floor.

ACTION:

1 Let the dumbbell hang by your side. Keeping your elbow close to your body, pull the dumbbell upward and back, until it almost touches your hip.
2 After you've 'rowed' the dumbbell back as far as it will go, slowly lower it to the start position.
3 After completing all your reps for this side, swap over and do the other side.

TIP

Don't hunch or round your back. Keep it flat.

TARGETS: FRONT OF UPPER ARMS

Biceps are the powerful lifting muscles of the upper arm. Keeping them strong adds great tone to your arms, and is very useful for picking up children and groceries!

START:

1 Sit with your arms by your sides, a dumbbell in each hand, palms facing forwards.
2 Take a deep breath and engage your trunk muscles.

ACTION:

1 Curl the dumbbells in towards your shoulders, keeping your upper arms firmly by your sides. Keep your torso still too – if you have to swing the weight to lift it, change to a lighter weight to make sure your biceps do all the work.
2 Lower the dumbbells slowly to the start point. Repeat before your elbow locks.

TIP

Don't lean forwards or backwards as you lower the weight – this takes work away from the biceps.

TARGETS: BACKS OF UPPER ARMS

These are the 'chicken wing' muscles which often wobble as we get older. Tighten them up for complete confidence in short sleeves.

START:

1 Rest your left knee and lower leg on one end of the bench and place your right hand on the other end.
2 Plant your right foot on the floor with the knee slightly bent.
3 Hold a dumbbell in your right hand, palm facing towards you.
4 Clamp your upper arm by the side of your body, so it's parallel with the floor. Bend your elbow so the weight dangles straight down.

ACTION:

1 Straighten your left arm slowly until it is almost fully extended. Don't lock your elbow. Your upper arm should stay in exactly the same position. Keep your back in the same, flat position.
2 Swing the lower arm slowly back to the start position.
3 After completing all your reps for this side, swap over and do the other side.

TIP

Don't let your torso twist as you lift. Keep your shoulders steady, facing straight down towards the floor.

the exercises

TARGETS: BUTTOCKS, TOP AND BACK OF THIGHS

If the bum is one of your worry zones, you'll love this exercise! Every time you push back to a standing position you can feel your glutes getting stronger. Remember – it won't 'spot reduce' fat on the bum, that's impossible, but it will firm the overall shape. If you find it hard, don't add dumbbells until week two.

START:

1 Stand with your feet shoulder-width apart, a dumbbell in each hand, arms by your sides.
2 Think about those stabilizing trunk muscles. Hold your spine in neutral, breathe in, keep your chest up and your abdominals tight.

ACTION:

1 Bend your knees and squat down, as though you were sitting down on a chair. Bend at the hips, so your shoulders, back and head keep the same line.
2 Allow your arms to dangle down so the dumbbells pass outside your knees.
3 Pushing from your heels, raise yourself up to your starting position.

TIP

Keep your spine and neck in line throughout this exercise, and don't forget to stick that tail out!

TARGETS: CALF

Many women worry about big calves but you use these muscles whenever you stand up, so they are unlikely to grow any more. Training will just make them stronger and your legs more shapely. If you find it hard, don't add dumbbells until week two or even later.

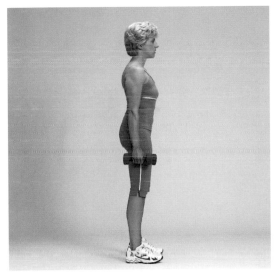 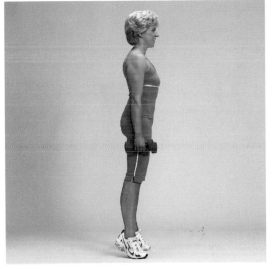

START:

1 Stand with your feet shoulder-width apart, a dumbbell in each hand.
2 Turn your toes out, so your feet form a 45 degree angle.
3 Take a deep breath and engage your trunk muscles to stabilize your upper body. Lift your chest and feel your spine take its neutral position.

ACTION:

1 Raise up on your toes as high as possible, stay there for the count of one.
2 Lower slowly to the start position. This puts a lot of stress on the Achilles tendon, so it must be slow for safety's sake.
3 After your repetitions, stretch the calf to keep it long and lean.

TIP

Don't do this exercise on carpet – find a solid surface like a hardwood or concrete floor.

the exercises

101

TARGETS: FRONT THIGHS AND BUTTOCKS

Along with squats, lunges are a key lower-body exercise. They work two important muscle groups at once while testing your balance, so all your trunk muscles get to work as well.

START:

1 Stand with your feet hip-width apart, toes pointing straight forward, a dumbbell in each hand. Rest the dumbbells on your hips if it helps you balance.

2 Breathe in and engage your trunk muscles; feel your abdominals tighten up. Keep your shoulders squared, chin up, back in neutral.

ACTION:

1 Take a big step forward with your left foot, allowing both knees to bend.

2 Lower your left knee towards the floor keeping your upper body straight.

3 At the deepest point of your lunge, your front thigh should be parallel with the floor and your knee over your ankle, so the leg makes a right angle.

4 Push through the front leg to raise yourself to the start position.

TIP

Learn this in front of a mirror, as the correct position can be hard to find. Remember to point both feet forward.

home workout

If you want to do your resistance exercises at home, you only need one piece of equipment: a resistance band. They're cheap, take barely any storage space, are effective and versatile. Some are colour-coded for different degrees of resistance but you can make exercises harder by shortening the length. Just wrap it an extra time around your hand or foot to make sure you always fatigue after 8–12 repetitions.

You'll find some of these harder than they look. Don't worry if you can't complete the full move. Just go as far as you can and return to the start position. It might help motivation if you use this as a goal in your training log: 'In four weeks, I will complete 12 full repetitions of this exercise.'

As the pull of the band can make you wobble around more than dumbbells, it's especially important to use your trunk muscles to hold yourself steady. Always take a second to breathe in before you start the action, and feel your abdominal and back muscles contract.

① Side arm raises

TARGETS: SHOULDERS

This surprisingly tough exercise will help to round your shoulders in the best possible way – by putting shapely 'caps' above your biceps.

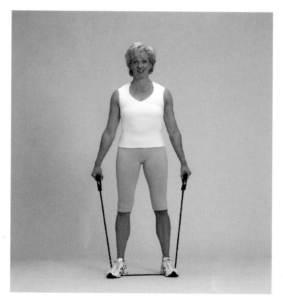 

START:

1 Stand with feet shoulder-width apart, one end of the band in each hand.
2 Slip a section of the band under one foot (or both feet, to make it really hard). Make sure it's positioned to give an even pull on both arms.
3 Keep your elbows slightly bent.
4 Breathe in and engage your trunk muscles. Relax your shoulders.

ACTION:

1 As you breathe out, lift your arms straight out to the side, as high as you can to shoulder height.
2 Breathe in as you slowly return your arms to the starting position.

TIP

Is the pull equal on both sides? Check at the top of your first rep. If one side is easier, adjust the band before the next repetition.

TARGETS: MIDDLE AND UPPER BACK

A strong back not only looks good, but is extremely functional! Using the muscles improves posture and can help correct back pain caused by hunching.

START:

1 Stand with your feet shoulder-width apart, one end of the resistance band in each hand.
2 Breathe in, engage your trunk muscles and check your spine is in neutral.

ACTION:

1 Hold your arms above your head, hands shoulder-width apart, a little tension in the band, elbows slightly bent.
2 Exhale as you pull your hands out and lower them in a sideways arc, until they come down to shoulder height.
3 Inhale as you return to the start position.

TIP

Keep your arms level with your chest or just in front, rather than stretched behind it.

the exercises

105

TARGETS: FRONT OF UPPER ARM

This tones the powerful lifting muscles of the upper arm. Madonna made them a fashion statement but they're also useful for toddlers and groceries!

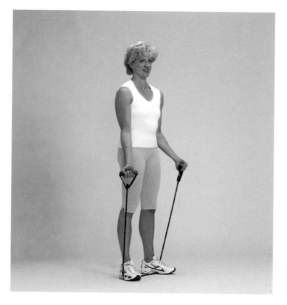

START:

1 Secure the resistance band under your feet, holding the ends in your hands.
2 Stand with your feet slightly wider than shoulder-width apart, arms by your sides, knees slightly bent.
3 Breathe in and engage your trunk muscles. Relax your shoulders.

ACTION:

1 Keeping your elbow tucked in by your waist, bend your arm at the elbow and curl your fist up to your shoulder. Breathe out as it curls up.
2 Return to start position, breathing in as you lower.
3 After your repetitions for this side, change and do the other side.

TIP

Keep that elbow tucked in!

TARGETS: SHOULDERS, TRICEPS

This works two muscles of the upper arm at once – great for those short-sleeved tops!

START:

1 If you need to increase tension, fold the resistance band in half.
2 Stand with your feet shoulder-width apart, one end of the band in each hand.
3 Lift the band to shoulder-height; stick your elbows out.
4 Breathe in and engage your trunk muscles. Relax your shoulders.

ACTION:

1 As you breathe out, extend your arms out to the side so the band stays about the same distance from your chest. Stop just before your elbows lock.
2 Breathe in as you return to the start position.

TIP

Lower the band so it's in line with your nipples and you've got a great chest exercise too!

the exercises

107

TARGETS: BACK OF UPPER ARM

This muscle gives your arms shape when they're by your sides. It responds quickly to exercise – so get cracking!

START:

1 Find a stable platform like the seat of a strong chair or step.
2 Sit on the edge of it. Grip the front or side edges with both hands.
3 Put your feet flat on the floor, legs slightly extended in front of you.
4 Wriggle forward so all your body weight is on your arms and feet.
5 Check your back is straight and your neck is in line with your spine.

ACTION:

1 Lower your bottom towards the floor by bending your arms.
2 Straighten your arms to lift back up. Stop just before your elbows lock.

TIP

To increase the intensity, keep your bottom close to the chair!

TARGETS: BACK OF UPPER THIGHS

Women tend to use the front of their thighs a lot while running. It's important to balance your strength by paying extra attention to the hamstrings.

START:

1 Fold the resistance band in half. Secure both handles around one foot or ankle.
2 On your hands and knees, secure the band under the instep of the working leg.
3 Rest your elbows on the floor, forearms in front of you. Extend the working leg and bend the knee, so your foot is raised.
4 Breathe in and pull in your abdominal muscles. Face the floor, your neck in line with your spine. Don't arch your back.

ACTION:

1 As you breathe out, lift up your working leg, keeping the knee bent.
2 Breathe in as you lower the working knee to an inch above the floor.
3 After completing your repetitions, swap to the other side.

TIP

Think about pushing your heel up to the ceiling. Don't twist your spine.

the exercises

109

TARGETS: BUTTOCKS, TOP AND BACK OF THIGHS

This simple action can have real impact on that notorious worry-zone, the back-side. Remember – it won't 'spot reduce' fat on the bum, that's impossible, but it will firm the overall shape.

START:

1 Stand with your feet hip-width apart, knees slightly bent, feet forward or turned out a little.
2 Put your hands on your hips or rest them on the tops of your thighs.
3 Breathe in and engage your trunk and buttock muscles. Hold your back in neutral, neck in line with your spine. Look straight ahead.

ACTION:

1 Breathe in again as you bend your knees and squat down. Your bum should stick out as though you were sitting on a chair. Bend at the hips, so your shoulders, back and head keep the same line.
2 When the legs reach an angle of 90 degrees, breathe out as you raise yourself up to your start position, pushing from your heels.

TIP

Your knees, thighs and the tips of your feet should stay in line throughout the movement. Don't forget to stick that tail out!

TARGETS: FRONT OF THIGHS

The quadriceps muscles are used every time you lift your leg, such as to walk or run. Keep them strong with this small but effective movement.

 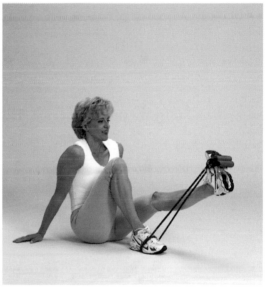

START:

1 Sit on the floor and secure both handles of the resistance band around one ankle.
2 Loop the middle of the band under the instep of your other foot.
3 Sit tall with both arms behind you, the working leg extended in front; the other knee should be bent, foot flat on the floor.
4 Breathe in and engage your trunk muscles.

ACTION:

1 As you breathe out, lift the working leg off the floor, keeping the knee soft.
2 Lower to just above the floor as you breathe in.

TIP

Relax your neck and shoulders – don't curl forward for that extra repetition!

the exercises

TARGETS: FRONT THIGHS AND BUTTOCKS

Lunges rank alongside squats as a top lower-body exercise. It works two important muscle groups at once while testing your balance, so all your trunk muscles get to work as well.

START:

1 Stand with your feet hip-width apart, toes pointing straight forward, knees slightly bent, hands on hips.
2 Breathe in and engage your trunk muscles. Keep your shoulders squared, chin up, back in neutral.

ACTION:

1 Take a big step forward with your left foot, allowing both knees to bend.
2 Lower your left knee towards the floor while keeping your upper body straight.
3 At the deepest point of your lunge, your front thigh should be parallel with the floor and your knee over your ankle, so the leg makes a right angle.
4 Push through the front leg to raise yourself to the start position.

be your best

TIP

Try learning this in front of a mirror.

abdominal exercises

The belly is a source of strife for many women, especially after the muscles have been stretched by pregnancy. If you remember to engage your trunk muscles during resistance exercise, this will help to strengthen the deepest layer of stomach muscles, the transversus abdominis. To work on the upper layers, you need to do specific abdominal exercises.

There are three sets of these muscles:

Rectus abdominis: Two strips of muscle running from your rib cage to your pubic bone. Both muscles have three separations, which produce the legendary six pack. The upper part is used to raise your shoulders off the floor; the lower part lifts your buttocks off the floor.

External obliques: A broad, thin muscle running diagonally from your ribs to your hips.

Internal obliques: These run along the front and sides of your torso. Internal and external obliques are used to bend to the side.

These muscles respond quickly to exercise, so you should feel an improvement within two weeks. After four weeks, you may see a difference, especially if your fat-burning strategies are working.

Working the abdominals won't, of course, directly reduce the fat layer on top of them, so there's no point doing 200 a day and ignoring the rest of the programme. However, as they become stronger, they're better able to hold in your stomach and other organs. That's when your waistline starts to re-emerge.

WHAT DO I INCLUDE?

After your resistance workout, do three sets of abdominal exercises: one for the upper rectus abdominis, one for the lower rectus abdominis and one for the obliques.

I've given you some options – you don't need to do them all! Variation is the key to improvement, so pick and mix each time you do them.

If possible, watch yourself do these in a mirror until you get the feel of them. They must be done correctly to work.

Always focus on the effect of your movements. Check it's your belly which does the work, never your back, shoulders or neck. Make the movements slow and controlled, so momentum can't do the work for you.

HOW DO I PROGRESS?

Start with the beginners' exercises. Once you can do 12 repetitions of those, try out some of the others. Increase the reps so you keep working until your muscles feel fatigued during each session.

Slow movements are much harder. If you zip through 40 without raising a sweat, you're wasting your time. Do them to the count of two up, two down, or four up, four down, or hold them at the top. Always focus on your abs and feel them contract.

TARGETS: UPPER RECTUS ABDOMINIS

Using the towel takes the strain off your neck – often a sore point when you start out.

START:

1 Lie on the towel so it's under your bum but above your head.
2 Bend your knees so your feet are flat on the floor, hip width apart.
3 Gently roll your head from side to side to release your neck.
4 Place the towel behind your neck and hold the corners with your hands above your head.

ACTION:

1 Breathe in and engage your trunk muscles.
2 Keep your eyes on the ceiling and lift your chin as though you were holding an orange under it. Lift your arms until the weight of your head is on the towel.
3 Breathe out, push your belly button towards your spine and lift your shoulder blades off the floor, raising the towel with your hands so it supports your head.
4 Breathe in as you slowly lower.

TIP

Keep that space under your chin!

the exercises

TARGETS: OBLIQUES

ACTION:

1 Breathe in and engage your trunk muscles. Lift your arms until the weight of your head is on the towel.

2 Breathe out, push your belly button towards your spine and lift your shoulder blades off the floor. Twist slightly so your left elbow heads towards your right knee. Don't strain the upper body, rely on the abs. Don't allow the pelvis to roll.

3 Breathe in as you slowly lower.

4 Alternate sides until your repetitions are complete.

TIP

The towel might help, but work your abs as much as you can.

③ Butt raises (beginner)

TARGETS: LOWER RECTUS ABDOMINIS

START:

1 Lie on your back, knees bent, spine straight. Check your spine is in neutral.
2 Put your hands on the floor, thumbs in the air so you can't push against them.
3 Raise your legs and bend your knees.
4 Breathe in and engage your trunk muscles.

ACTION:

1 Using your lower abs, lift your hips off the floor so your knees head towards your face.
2 Hold for a count of two.
3 Lower your hips in a slow and controlled motion, keeping your abs contracted until they're back on the floor.

TIP

For a slightly harder version, put your hands under your neck but take care not to pull on them.

TARGETS: OBLIQUES

START:

1 Stand with your feet shoulder-width apart, knees slightly bent.
2 Put your hands behind your head, elbows sticking out.
3 Breathe in, engage your trunk muscles and check your spine is in neutral.

ACTION:

1 Focus on your oblique muscles and use them to bend to your right side in a slow, controlled movement. Your right elbow should be heading towards your right knee.
2 Return to the start position and repeat to the same side until you have completed your repetitions.
3 Perform the exercise on the opposite side.

TIP

Pretend you're sandwiched between two panes of glass, so you don't lean forwards or back.

⑤ Arms up butt raises

TARGETS: LOWER RECTUS ABDOMINIS

START:

1 Lie on your back, knees bent, spine straight. Check your spine is in neutral.
2 Raise your arms and hold on to a secure object, such as the legs of a heavy armchair or desk.
3 Raise your legs straight up, keeping your knees soft.
4 Breathe in and engage your trunk muscles.

ACTION:

1 Using your lower abs, raise your hips off the floor and lift your knees in towards your face.
2 Lower your legs until your hips touch the floor.

TIP

Don't use your arms or shoulders to help, and beware of momentum.

fitness
fuel

eating for health

You might expect an ex-international athlete to be eternally virtuous about food. If it's a lettuce leaf evangelist you're after – don't look at me! I love crisps. I'm not mad keen on vegetables. I have to do regular sit-ups to control my tummy. I eat certain foods because I know they improve my health and wellbeing, but I love exercise because it means I can eat lots of other things too.

Food is no longer a big thing in my life. It's sociable, enjoyable, but it doesn't dominate every waking moment. In fact, I'm happy to say my relationship with food has reached a pleasant equilibrium.

It's a huge improvement on the mid-Eighties, when weird eating was the order of the day. I worked part-time as a nanny near my home in Essex and sweets, fish fingers and chips were a way of life. If the two kids I looked after didn't eat it, I did; it was pick, pick, pick all day. When Jon first met me in 1985, he thought I was a shot putter! At the time I lined up for the 100m hurdles in the Commonwealth Games I was one and a half stone heavier than my ideal race weight. One and a half stone! I won gold, though I'm not sure how I did it – I must have rolled over the hurdles.

Because I was performing well, no-one said anything about my weight, which was probably a good thing – I worried about it enough as it was. Or, I would have a slimmer's shake for breakfast, another for lunch and spend the whole day praying for dinner.

I tried every kind of diet from every book and magazine. I would skip breakfast, have a tiny lunch, then gorge myself in the evening.

I counted calories until I saw food as a series of numbers. I cut fat and craved it tenfold. No matter which routine it was, after seven or maybe 10 days (if I did really well) I'd have a packet of crisps and think, 'That's ruined it', and abandon myself to misery and bad habits.

Apart from making me needlessly guilty and depressed, this style of eating failed to provide the energy I needed for my training. What's more, it didn't do anything for my body shape at all. It was worse than pointless – it was harmful. And here's me, an athlete who had invested all her hopes and dreams in the performance of her body! It was like Michael Schumacher filling the tank of his F1 racing car with water.

I'd like to say that I suddenly came to my senses and decided to respect and help my body rather than torture and punish it – but I didn't. I did, however, change from the 100m to the 400m hurdles, an event which demanded a different style of training. The longer runs demanded more of my aerobic system and I felt a need for more nutritious fuel. Without even realizing it, I cut out the mad diets and started to consistently eat better food. That cut my craving for crisps straight away. I gave up mixing drink powders, weighing food and counting calories, which set me free from a vicious cycle: fiddling about with food made me think about it more (especially what I couldn't have), which made me want it more and enjoy eating less. I only thought of calories instead of flavour, so the pleasure of whatever I put in my mouth was wasted.

I began to eat as much as I wanted, so long as it was healthy.

Before I knew it, I'd lost a few pounds. More importantly, food was no longer the be-all-and-end-all, it was just another part of my very busy life, and had certainly lost its power over my mood and self-esteem.

fitness fuel

In 1992, my relationship with food went in the opposite direction from my slimmer's shake days. Gearing up for the Olympics, I knew the difference between winning and losing came down to tiny parts of a second, and I wanted everything possible to be on my side. I visited sports nutritionist Eric Llewellyn, who was a champion of organic foods long before they came to supermarkets. He told me to make my food as pure as possible, so my body didn't have to fight against it. Jon and I had to scour the country to find organic chicken, organic fruit, organic vegetables, organic pasta and rice. I ate nothing with additives and hardly anything sweet.

Still, I wasn't a total obsessive. During winter training, when it's more important to build a base level of strength and fitness than refine your speed, I still ate the odd Mars bar or crisps. Eric said if I craved something, it was because I needed it. Jon says it was like living with a pregnant woman: if I wanted a Snickers at 10 o'clock at night, we had to go out and find a Snickers – fast.

I allowed myself occasional Chinese take-away too – another favourite of mine – but as I immersed myself in Eric's diet, my taste for them dwindled. Once his pure food became normal, I was more sensitive to the effects of heavy food and additives. In the end, I knew I'd feel so lethargic and sluggish the next day they no longer seemed appetizing to me, let alone a treat.

In the six months before the Olympics, there was no chance of it anyway. No junk, no sweet things, no excuses. I wanted to stand alongside the best hurdlers in the world and know inside myself that I'd done everything I could to beat them.

This eating style had a big impact on my mind and body. I was awake to the effects certain foods had on how I felt and performed. For the first time, I had more trouble keeping weight on than keeping it off. When other women asked what I ate, they were impressed by the quantities I devoured. They thought that to be skinny, I must be living on carrot sticks – of course it's possible to eat and enjoy loads of tasty food while staying in great shape, but this often hit them as a major revelation.

These days, my eating style is comfortably balanced between my past extremes. I enjoy natural, healthy food, plus a few packets of crisps a week. I enjoy going out and the social side of food more than anything, I'm not obsessed by it at all. I look forward to my evening meal because I'm going to catch up with friends and family, not because I'll finally be allowed to eat.

can the can'ts

A personal best isn't about what you can't do. 'Wow, I've made it, I can't eat sponge cake!' Not particularly exciting, is it? No, a personal best is about what you can do. When you start an exercise programme, you get an instant raft of 'can do's'. You can do weight training, you can run further than you could last week, you can try wind surfing or basketball. It's this I want you to concentrate on, and try not to worry about 'can't'. The more you achieve 'can's', the better you feel about yourself, and the more inclined you are to do more. However, as soon as you eat a 'can't' (or a 'shouldn't' or a 'mustn't'), the more you feel like a failure. That makes you want to chuck the whole thing away, as I did umpteen times in my diet-crazy days.

So don't obsess about food. The extra exercise you do is enough to help you start losing weight. As you start to feel fitter and healthier, you may want to speed up the results by reevaluating your diet as well. I know that after I've been training, I don't particularly want to blow it all on a chocolate pig-out – all that effort would have been for nothing! Even after a big race, I used to promise myself chips, sausages and double helpings of pudding but when I finally sat down to eat it, I was usually disappointed. I felt vibrant and alive, and just looking at all that stuff made me feel bleugh!

So focus on your fitness and let your diet find its own balance. Be aware of the way food affects body shape but don't get wound up about it. Just accept responsibility for whatever you put in your mouth – you're a grown adult with a fistful of choices; the buck stops with you.

Oh no, is that chocolate bar calling out to you again, 'pleeeease eat me'?

how can i resist?

1. Look it in the eye. Do you really, honestly want it, or is it an excuse? Do something else for 15 minutes; if you still crave it, eat and enjoy.
2. Offer yourself a piece of fruit first. If you don't want it, you're not hungry; if you do eat the fruit, you probably won't want the chocolate bar any more.
3. Swap it for a lower-calorie version with a similar taste, such as a chocolate chip cereal bar (not a flapjack – some commercial ones are massively high in fat) or an individual chocolate mousse.
4. Find other solutions to the bored/lonely/deserving quandary. Have an aromatherapy bath, ring a friend, give yourself that pat on the back.
5. Don't buy it in the first place. Just don't!
6. It's not a choice between now or never. If you open a packet of biscuits, take a couple and put the rest back, secure in the knowledge they'll still be there tomorrow.
7. Really, really taste what you eat. If you shut your eyes and focus on the flavours of chocolate inside your mouth, you may discover the intense sweetness and claggy texture isn't as delicious as you assumed.
8. Brush your teeth, chew gum or drink peppermint tea. That clean, minty flavour stays in the mouth and can make chocolate seem less appealing.

how can i instantly improve my diet – without suffering?

Some changes take a few days to get used to but stick with it – you'll suffer a lot less in the long run.

1. Think carbohydrates first. Pasta, rice, potatoes, cereals, pulses, noodles, cous cous or bread should make the basis of your meal. Augment with good helpings of vegetables, then add protein, such as meat, fish or tofu, last of all.

2. Steam vegetables. Put them in a pan with just a quarter inch of water, put a lid on and cook on a medium heat for a few minutes. The vegetables keep their flavour, nutrients and bright colours. Even better, buy a trivet, a type of collapsible colander which keeps the vegetables above the water, preserving maximum goodness.

3. Watch your portions. Give yourself two thirds of your normal helping. Once you've finished, sit back and relax for a minute. If you're really not full, have some leftovers, or put them in the fridge in case you suddenly feel starving. If you don't, throw them away and cook less next time.

4. Aim for five portions of different fruit and veg a day (see p14 for portion sizes). This can include one juice, one helping of dried fruit, frozen and canned versions, but not potatoes (they're too starchy and count as carbohydrate), nuts or seeds.

5. Use little or no fat during cooking. Grill fatty foods like sausages and bacon on a rack (a sheet of foil over the baking tray saves cleaning later). Meat, fish and vegetables can be oven baked with maybe a light brushing of olive oil, or wrapped plain in tin foil to be kept moist.

6. Use mature cheddar – the stronger flavour means you need less. Grate it and it goes even further.

7. Drink skimmed milk. If you currently drink whole milk, change to semi-skimmed until you're ready for the final leap.

8. Eat multi-purpose foods. Choose cereals with fibre and extra vitamins, bread with seeds and grains, puddings with fruit in them and you'll do better than just fill a hole.

9. Avoid adding fat for presentation, such as butter on vegetables or high fat salad dressing. Use fromage frais or yoghurt on a baked potato, and low-calorie versions of dressings.

10. Watch the olive oil. Although it's famously better for you than most fats and oils, it's still a fat, so don't go wild.

fitness fuel

127

... bones?

Calcium is the essential mineral for strong bones, and also improves heart and muscle function. You don't have to eat a lot of high fat dairy products to get it; go for skimmed milk, low-fat cheese and yoghurt, oily fish canned with their bones, almonds, spinach and sesame seeds. Vitamin D is needed to absorb the calcium. This is plentiful in herrings, mackerel, tuna, sardines – and sunshine! Try to eat calcium-rich foods separate from foods which can inhibit absorption, such as wheat bran, whole grains, spinach, chard, rhubarb, beetroot, chocolate, tea and coffee.

... muscles?

Body builders go mad on raw eggs (gee thanks, Rocky), because protein is important for cell maintenance and repair. All things in moderation though – research suggests we only need 10 to 15 per cent of our calories from protein and too much – especially animal protein – is bad for kidneys and bones in the long term. A balanced diet with lots of carbohydrates, fruit and vegetables is a better bet. Selenium-rich foods like Brazil nuts, lentils and tuna in brine, plus supplements like selenium, vitamin E and Evening Primrose oil, may help with muscle pain.

... the immune system?

A good diet is a strong defence against bugs. Even once you've got flu or a cold, foods rich in vitamins A, C and E can help.

Vitamin A-rich foods: carrots, spinach, cantaloupe melon, sunflower seeds, avocado, squash, mango, broccoli, tomatoes.

Vitamin C-rich foods: citrus fruit, blackcurrants, berries, melon, red pepper, broccoli, leafy green vegetables.

Vitamin E-rich foods: sunflower seeds, sweet potato, avocado, chickpeas, Brazil nuts, salmon, squash, kale, tuna.

... depressed moods?

When you feel down, soft, rich, chocolatey foods suddenly become your best friends. These do release the natural happy-drug – seratonin – into the brain but there are alternatives. Oily fish like tuna, sardines and mackerel contain omega-3 fatty acids, which are scientifically linked with levels of depression. Vitamin B keeps the nervous system in tune (try Quorn, Marmite, Special K, tuna, or vegetable paté). Bright colours are also proven mood enhancers, so go for a cheerful stir fry of broccoli, tomatoes, yellow peppers and mange tout or a fruit salad with strawberries and melon.

... all-day energy?

Quick-release energy foods like sugar and chocolate make you feel up one minute, down the next. For sustained energy throughout the day, choose carbohydrate foods which release energy gradually over a few hours, like baked beans, rye bread, potatoes, porridge, pasta, noodles, kiwi-fruit, apples, dried apricots, grapefruit, mango and oranges.

how can i make healthy food taste nice?

If you make small, gradual changes, you shouldn't even notice your improved diet, let alone resent it, but these tips might help.

1. Sell it to yourself. Reorganize the way you think about food and give yourself lots of positive images to feed off. When you visit the fruit and veg department, think crunchy, munchy, juicy, yummy. Look at the amazing colours and shapes, feel the variety of textures. Put up gorgeous pictures in your kitchen of freshly harvested vegetables, kissed with morning dew.
2. Use your taste buds. If you've never steamed vegetables before, try them plain a few times. They really do have amazing flavour – not like the bland, soggy veg of old.
3. Experiment. Buy a new book of healthy recipes and find out how to treat the unusual fruit and veg now commonly available in supermarkets, such as fennel, okra, Swiss chard, passion fruit, star fruit and ugli fruit.
4. Use herbs and sauces. Fresh herbs (bought or grown at home) can transform a dish, but keep a dried selection on standby too. A dash of sauce or spice can give exotic flavour to a simple dish. Have you tried oyster sauce, soya sauce, hot chilli sauce, anchovy essence, cajun seasoning or Chinese five spice?
5. Add a few strongly flavoured items to a vegetable stir-fry or tomato-based pasta sauce, such as olives, sun-dried tomatoes, pieces of feta cheese, bits of lean bacon, sunflower seeds or garnish with a spoon of natural yoghurt.

what about snacking?

If you feel peckish during the day, snacking is fine to keep your energy-levels constant. There's loads of small, healthy nibbles to enjoy – in fact, snacking is a good way to boost your five a day intake of fruit and vegetables. Why not adjust your breakfast so you feel hungry enough to have two pieces of fruit during the morning? Knowing there's something healthy you can eat whenever you want is a freedom you'll come to appreciate, so keep a store of appetizing snacks at work or in the kitchen, such as:

Kid-sized boxes of raisins, dried apricots, sesame breadsticks, low fat cereal bars, blueberry bagels, crumpets, crisp bread, low-fat yoghurt, plus of course an attractive bowl of fresh fruit.

i eat healthily – why do i still put on weight?

If you eat healthy food in the right quantities, you can't put on weight. Something isn't adding up, so check:

1. Is your food truly healthy? Some items could be made with more fat than you thought. Watch out for fat traps like:
   cream crackers
   shop-bought flapjacks
   vegetable pasties (veggies are good, but all pastry except filo is high in fat)
   croissants (made with tonnes of butter)
   toasted muesli (very heavy – choose a non-toasted, no added sugar variety)
   egg mayonnaise sandwiches (sliced boiled eggs are much better)
   vegeburgers (usually high in fat)
   'low fat' food which is very high in sugar

For a quick impression of a food's fat content, place it on a sheet of paper. If it leaves transparent, greasy marks behind, that's fat.

2. Not sure what's healthy any more? You're always safe if it doesn't come with a label! Pure food is safer and more filling than processed food.
3. 'Vegetarian' doesn't always mean healthy. Change cream sauces for tomato-based sauces, don't over-do the cheese toppings and be wary of sugar and salt content in ready-meals.
4. Be honest. Keep a food diary for a week and you will probably discover more extra nibbles than you realized. Consciously swapping them for fruit or having three nutritious meals a day will make a big difference.
5. Check your quantities. Only eat your food, not your kids' or your partner's. Your body is not a rubbish bin.

why didn't my other diets work?

GOING WITHOUT:

Many dieters skip breakfast, have a tiny lunch and totally pig-out in the evening. No wonder – you're starving! By the time you finally allow yourself to eat, you'll gorge yourself on the first things available, usually fast, convenient, high-fat food. The overall effect is poor nutrition and a confused metabolism which has slowed down to protect you from starvation. Regular meals with plenty of slow-release carbohydrates will vastly improve your weight loss programme.

FOOD COMBINING:

On this diet, you can't eat protein (such as fish, meat, eggs) during the same meal as carbohydrate (pasta, bread, potatoes). The theory is the foods aren't properly digested if eaten together, leading to weight problems. Karen, on our Personal Best Team, had good results on this diet but there's no scientific evidence to prove protein fights carbohydrate – in fact some foods, like beans and potatoes, contain both. It could be that the rules are so strict and complex, you simply end up eating less. It works, but it's unnecessarily difficult.

CABBAGE-SOUP DIET

Many diets claim the wondrous effects of eating one type of food – for a while, the trendy thing was cabbage soup. While people seem able to exist for an amazingly long time on a monotone diet (remember the boy who ate nothing but jam sandwiches?) it can never give your body all the nutrients it needs. Weight loss may occur because your calorie intake is reduced but it surrenders all your choice and responsibility. Variety is the spice of life and any one food gets boring after a while – even jam sandwiches!

VERY LOW-FAT DIET

Cutting saturated fat is a healthy idea, but fats are still an important part of our diet. Healthy fats are found in nuts, plant oil and oily fish, so it's important not to cut them out completely. Small amounts of added fat also make food taste better and can help you feel satiated after a meal. If you can stick it, fine, but most people get a sense of deprivation which is eventually overcome by a choc-fest.

MEAL REPLACEMENT

It's those shakes again! True, they don't taste too bad and the idea of a creamy shake twice a day is fairly appetizing at first. I lasted at least nine days on this one but after a while, the mixing and monotony was too much. Besides, it's not proper food! Surely it's a better investment for life to learn about healthy eating and permit yourself to enjoy good food.

HIGH-PROTEIN DIET (THE ZONE DIET)

A difficult one from an athlete's point of view, because members of the US swimming team on this diet won gold in the Barcelona and Atlanta Olympics. You're supposed to get 40 per cent of your calories from protein, 30 per cent from carbohydrates and 30 per cent from fat, whereas normal recommendations are about 15, 50 and 35 per cent respectively. You may lose weight with it simply because calories are restricted, and it's not easy to find snacks which fit the formula. It obviously works for some people but somehow, I would stick to a conventional balance until more is known about this combination, especially as research suggests excessive protein strains the kidneys.

CARBOHYDRATE-FREE DIET

A handful of celebrities recently popularized the idea of cutting carbohydrates to a minimum. We heard all about their weight loss but nothing about the side-effects – I suspect they would have been low on energy, tired and unproductive. There's no denying carbohydrates are the best form of low-fat, slow release energy and if you exercise, you need them. Be Your Personal Best team-member Pam actually tried this during the first week of her exercise programme but quickly gave up when it brought her active lifestyle to a juddering halt.

CALORIE COUNTING

Cutting calories works – it must do. If you eat less calories than you burn off, you'll lose weight. The thing is, life is too short. And food is too delicious. Converting everything to numbers takes the joy out of eating – eat healthy food, exercise regularly and you shouldn't have to be this obsessive. However, if you haven't thought much about the food you eat before, it wouldn't hurt to develop an awareness of what's in it.

what should i drink?

1. Water. You've probably heard the rumour about how much water you're supposed to drink – it's true! Two litres, every day, more if you exercise. It's a shock at first but after a couple of weeks, you'll awaken your natural sense of thirst and it will become much easier. The number of trips to the loo should also even out! I have a large glass of water when I wake up and a glass with each meal, so that's half of it taken care of. The rest I only remember to drink if I have a glass or bottle of water near me, so if you spend a lot of time in one place, say at your desk, keep a large bottle there and work your way through it.

2. Juice. Fruit and vegetable juices became part of my daily life when I was preparing for the Olympics. It's such a convenient way to ingest their nutrients that I've kept it up ever since – it's terrific for a non-veggie fanatic! You get everything except the fibre, so it's not the complete solution but it's a delicious help.

3. Hot water. I have a glass first thing every morning, with honey and lemon because I love zesty flavours. This was another of Eric's tips, and it really helps to cleanse the system.

4. Tea, coffee, cola? I drank loads of tea until recently, when I decided I was addicted and cut down to one mug a day. I feel much better for it, and it's made me drink more water too. The general guide is that up to five cups a day is okay but remember that they're diuretic, so you end up losing more liquid than you gain, which means you need to drink more water. Cola drinks add more sugar and/or additives to the diet. I'd swap them for water if at all possible.

Because this programme is about what you can do, not what you can't, I'm not giving the Team any radical diet sheets to follow. However, a couple of small alterations can make a big difference, especially when they back-up regular exercise.

Alison

- ◆ likes a fried breakfast because she works outside
- ◆ chocoholic – up to five bars a day!

I don't believe in banning any type of food, but Alison's chocolate addiction is sabotaging her whole diet. Who would feel like a filling, nutritious evening meal after such a calorific day at work?

The change will work better if it occurs gradually, and if the snacks are replaced with something else. As she has good motivation to change, she may be able to say right, no chocolate bars until after lunch. When she gets the munchies during the morning, she should have a sweet, healthy snack like an apple, satsuma or a small box of raisins. She could have chocolate as normal during the afternoon, or swap in a choc-chip cereal bar. If she bulks up her main meal in the evening with a large helping of pasta, potatoes or rice, she may feel too full to bother with more snacks.

A fried breakfast a couple of times a week isn't a huge problem. All she needs to do is reduce the saturated fat: grill bacon and tomatos instead of frying them, skip the sausage, have beans instead of fried mushrooms and fry the egg in a non-stick pan with only a light brush of oil or poach it instead.

Lucy

Business lunches are difficult to avoid if they're part of your job. Lucy regularly visits the same area, so she should track down a few cafés and restaurants with a selection of light, healthy foods and suggest going there for lunch. She should choose dishes which aren't fried or cooked in a creamy sauce. Chicken salad, grilled fish or baked potato with tuna are good. She could also try:

◆ a light entree such as melon and ham.
◆ a starter-sized main meal and a side-salad.
◆ only small amounts of pasta, so she doesn't feel sleepy all afternoon.
◆ drinking water, never alcohol.
◆ ordering tea or espresso instead of pudding.

As for the biscuits, if she can't help buying them, she should buy Garibaldis, fig rolls or Jaffa Cakes, which are relatively low in saturated fat. Again, she should learn to listen to her tummy and only eat when she's hungry. If vegetable portions are low, raw carrots make a good snack!

Karen

It's those pesky kids again! Young children can make it so hard to stick to your own, sensible diet. Karen could

◆ scrape those leftovers straight into the bin.
◆ give her children smaller portions if they don't eat a lot.
◆ snack on fruit before she meets friends, so she's less hungry for crisps or ice-cream. Only buy them if she really wants to eat them, not out of habit or social obligation.
◆ encourage the children to join her in eating more of her 'grown up' food. I know it's really hard once they've got a taste for fast food but I can usually persuade Finley to eat what we eat. Trips to McDonald's are rare, so he knows they're a treat for special occasions.
◆ keep healthy snacks handy for when she's giving the children their tea, such as raisins, dried apricots or a toasted bagel.

Neil

Portions, portions, portions. Neil is a big eater; his wife isn't. He rushes through his meal and looks forward to finishing hers. No more! He should try to eat more slowly, so his stomach has time to digest the food he's put into it and for the messages of fullness to reach his brain. He must learn to scrape leftovers into the bin or let the waiter take them away. If he really is still hungry, he should boost his fruit intake after dinner.

Since Neil's fruit intake is so low and he's worried about bad food eaten on business trips, he should always take a goody-bag of healthy snacks in the car. Apples and bananas travel well and can be eaten while driving.

Pam

The hot flushes of menopause are unknown to women in China and Japan because their high levels of soya-based foods really help. Pam should boost her intake of tofu and calcium-enriched soya-milk, plus try yams, linseed, bean sprouts and other fresh vegetables.

As metabolism naturally decreases with age, she may simply need less calories. Cutting back on all processed food would help with this and help any fluid retention, as many are high in salt. She should drink only decaffeinated tea and coffee, and make sure she gets plenty of water or fresh juice. Her regular snacks should include nuts, seeds, fresh or dried fruit, fortified soya milk and rye crispbread.

recipes
for success

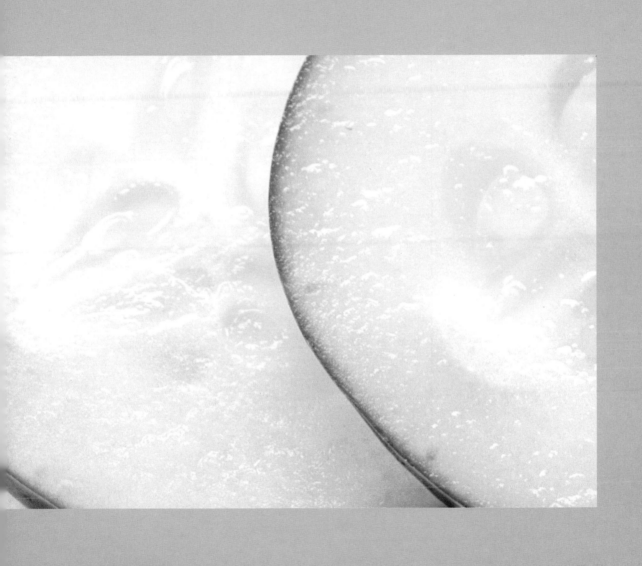

Breakfast eaters consistently show better concentration and performance than non-breakfast eaters. They're also less likely to crave fatty snacks at morning tea! I never skip it because it sets me up for the day and boosts my daily fibre and fruit intake.

power porridge (1 serving)

2oz/50g/½ cup porridge oats
¼ pint (150ml) water
¼ pint (150ml) skimmed/non-fat milk
handful of dried fruit, such as sultanas, chopped apricots, chopped apple rings
½ chopped, fresh banana (optional)
1 tsp honey (optional)

1. Place oats in a small saucepan, then add the liquid. You can alter the proportions of water to milk if you like it more or less creamy.
2. Bring to the boil.
3. Lower heat and simmer for 3–5 minutes, stirring occasionally.
4. Add the dried fruit, stir and pour into a serving bowl. Add the chopped bananas and honey on top if desired.

A film of porridge always sticks to the saucepan after you've poured it out. Pour cold water on it and leave for a few minutes, then you can tip off the water, scoop out the gloop and drop it in the bin.

For larger quantities, the general rule is one part oats to two or two-and-a-half parts liquid.

For super-speed, use the microwave. Put oats and liquid in a large serving bowl and blast for two minutes. Stir and cook another 1–1½ minutes. Add fruit and extra skimmed milk if required.

super muesli (6 servings)

3oz/75g/¾ cup porridge oats

3oz/75g/¾ cup barley flakes

2oz/50g/½ cup wheat flakes

1oz/25g/¼ cup oat bran

1oz/25g/¼ cup raisins

1oz/25g/¼ cup dried apricots

1oz/25g/¼ cup chunky-chopped Brazil nuts

Skimmed/non-fat milk, to serve

Fresh fruit, such as grated apple or banana chunks, to serve

Low-fat yoghurt (optional)

1. Combine all the dry ingredients and store in an air tight jar.
2. When you get up in the morning, pour a serving into a bowl and cover in skimmed milk. Leave to stand for at least 15 minutes, while you get dressed (or do your Sun Salutations – see p158).
3. Add the fresh fruit and a dollop of yoghurt.

power juices

A juicer gives you a world of fantastic concoctions to explore. We have at least one juice every day – it's a delicious way to add one good serving of fruit or veg to your daily tally. Some nutritionists say you should stick to either fruit or vegetable juices in the one glass (to reduce the risk of embarrassing wind), although apple and carrot go well with everything.

PERFECT PEAR

4 pears
12 seedless grapes, black or white
2 apples
2 slices pineapple

1. Slice the outer skin off the pineapple.
2. Chop the pears, apples and pineapple into juice-able slices. Don't bother to peel or core the pears or apples, just wash and de-seed them.
3. Juice!

BRAIN BUZZ

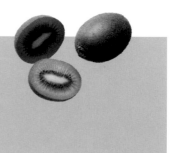

4 carrots
1 kiwi fruit
1 apple
handful of parsley

1. Peel the carrots and chop off the tops and tails (unless they're organic). Peel the kiwi fruit. Wash chop and de-seed the apple, leaving it with core and skin.
2. Juice!

super smoothies

If you don't have a juicer, maybe you have a blender? Inexpensive hand-held versions can pulverize soft fruit or vegetables like spinach, berries, satsumas, peaches and kiwi fruit, creating colourful and nutritious smoothies.

GREEN DREAM

1 bunch spinach (or watercress for a more peppery flavour)
2 tomatoes
½ an avocado
1 sprig of fresh oregano, chopped.

1. Mash the avocado. Tear the spinach or watercress into smaller pieces, removing any thick stems. Roughly chop the tomatoes and oregano.
2. Pulverize together, adding each ingredient separately.

TROPICAL VIBE

½ medium pineapple
1 orange
1 banana
Low-fat, natural yoghurt
1 tsp of honey
Skimmed/non-fat milk

1. Peel the pineapple and chop into small pieces. Peel the orange and banana.
2. Blend the pineapple and orange pieces. (Some hand-held blenders have a metal mesh cup, which helps you push out the juice and leave the chewy bits behind.)
3. Add the chopped banana, yoghurt and honey, plus skimmed milk to reach the right consistency.

BERRY DELICIOUS

6oz/150g/1½ cups of strawberries or other berry fruit
1 satsuma
115ml skimmed/non-fat milk

Either

1 Weetabix/Shredded Wheat
Low-fat natural yoghurt

Or

1 scoop of ice cream
Crushed ice

1.   Peel the satsuma; rinse and prepare the berries. Blend together. Add the milk.

FOR A BREAKFAST IN A GLASS:

2a.   Crush the Weetabix or Shredded Wheat and add, along with a dollop of yoghurt. Blend.

FOR A MOMENT'S MAD LUXURY:

2b.   Add the ice cream and crushed ice. Blend.

Lunch usually has to be the no-fuss meal of the day. You can make healthy sandwiches and salads in the morning or the night before if you keep a stock of essentials, such as wholemeal bread or buns (in the freezer), a bag of ready-prepared salad, a few tomatoes, an avocado, a tin of tuna in brine, red peppers and eggs (for boiling and slicing).

If you'd like to make something which can be kept and used throughout the week, try these two:

bean 'n' basil spread

This low-fat spread can be used as a sandwich filling or a dip for raw vegetables.

1 14oz (400g) tin of cannellini or butter beans
1 clove of garlic
1 tbsp olive oil
2 tsps lemon juice
salt and pepper
1 good sprig of fresh basil leaves

1. Drain and rinse the beans. Crush the garlic.
2. Place everything except the basil in a blender or food processor and whiz until it's like a rough paté. Alternatively, mash with a potato masher (it's a good workout).
3. Tear or chop the basil leaves into small pieces. Mix them in with a fork and give it a very quick blend or mash.
4. Store in an airtight container in the fridge.

butternut soup (serves 2)

Butternut squash is plentiful in winter and full of goodness including antioxidants, vitamin C and vitamin E. You can make this soup with pumpkin if you prefer. Double the quantities and you can keep some in the fridge to heat up later.

½ butternut squash
1 onion
½ pint/300ml/1½ cups vegetable stock (bouillon)
1 tsp nutmeg

1. Scoop the seeds out of the butternut and discard. You need to peel the skin off – either do this now if you have a steady hand and a sharp knife, or wash it and wait until the end of step 3. It comes off easily when the squash is cooked but it's very hot to handle!
2. Cut the butternut into flat chunks and dice the onion.
3. Put the vegetables in a large frying pan. Cook on a very low heat with the lid on. Allow them to 'sweat' until the butternut is soft – 15–25 minutes, depending on size of chunks.
4. If necessary, take out the butternut and peel off the skin. Return to pan.
5. Mash the vegetables with a potato masher and add the stock. Simmer for another 10 minutes.
6. Add the nutmeg, plus salt, pepper and skimmed milk to taste.

To me, dinner is a time to socialize and catch up, not cook or do dishes! Fast food takes on a new (healthy) meaning with recipes like these.

chicken & broccoli stir fry (serves 4)

12oz/350g/3 cups boneless chicken

1 tbsp cornflour

1 tbsp soy saucep

1 tbsp sherry (optional)

12oz/350g/3 cups broccoli

1 tbsp vegetable oil

2 garlic cloves, chopped

2 tbsps fresh root ginger, finely chopped or grated

4 tbsps water

2 tbsps hoisin sauce (optional)

1. Slice chicken into thin strips.
2. In a bowl, stir together cornflour, soy sauce and sherry. Add chicken and stir to coat well.
3. Cut broccoli into florets.
4. Heat oil in a large, non-stick frying pan or wok. Use a high heat. Add the chicken mixture and stir fry for two minutes or until lightly browned.
5. Stir in garlic, ginger and broccoli. Stir fry for two more minutes.
6. Add water, cover and steam for two minutes or until broccoli is tender. Stir in hoisin sauce.
7. Serve over hot noodles or rice.

teriyaki orange fish fillets (serves 4)

1lb/450g/4 cups fish fillets, such as cod, sole, haddock

Rind and juice of one large orange

½ small onion, finely chopped

1 tbsp soy sauce

1 tsp fresh root ginger, grated

½ tsp sugar

1 tbsp water

1 tsp cornflour

1. Arrange fish in a single layer in a large frying pan.
2. In a small bowl, mix the orange rind and juice, onion, soy sauce, ginger and sugar. Pour it over the fish.
3. Bring to a boil. Reduce heat, cover and simmer for 3–5 minutes, or until the fish is opaque and flakes easily with a fork.
4. Use a fish slice to take out the fillets and put them on the serving plates.
5. Mix the cornflour and water in the small bowl until smooth, then pour into the pan with the fish juice. Bring to the boil while stirring.
6. Once the sauce is thickened, pour over the fish. Serve with green vegetables and rice or noodles.

mediterranean pasta (serves 4)

10oz/300g/2 ½ cups pasta such as penne, macaroni or shells

1 tbsp olive oil

1 clove garlic, chopped

4 large tomatoes, cut in wedges

16 black olives, halved

2oz/50g/½ cup crumbled Feta cheese

Fresh parsley and basil, chopped or 2 tsps dried basil

Grated Parmesan cheese

1. Put the pasta on to boil in a large saucepan.
2. Heat oil in a large, non-stick frying pan over medium heat.
3. Stir in the garlic. Add tomatoes and cook for three minutes, stirring frequently.
4. Once the pasta is cooked and drained, add the tomato mixture. Add olives, Feta and herbs, tossing gently to mix.
5. Sprinkle with Parmesan and serve with a large mixed salad.

summer fruit celebration

Summer berries taste so good I'm amazed they're healthy as well! Strawberries and blackcurrants are stuffed full of vitamin C, while raspberries are a good source of fibre.

7oz/200g/2 cups strawberries
3½oz/100g/1 cup raspberries
3½oz/100g/1 cup blackcurrants
1 tbsp sugar
1 cinnamon stick
3 tbsps water
dash of lemon juice
Greek-style yoghurt or ice-cream

1. Preheat the oven to 160° C/325° F/Gas 3.
2. Prepare the fruit, rinsing the blackcurrants and strawberries.
3. Place the berries, sugar and cinnamon stick in a shallow baking dish with the water. Cover and bake for 30 minutes, stirring gently once. The fruit should be soft, with a rich juice.
4. Remove the cinnamon stick and stir in the lemon juice. Serve with yoghurt or ice cream.

be your best

apple & banana fingers

If you need a sweet treat (and who doesn't), these slices have carbohydrate and fibre to help shrug off any remnants of guilt. I sometimes freeze them and defrost at room temperature for an hour as needed.

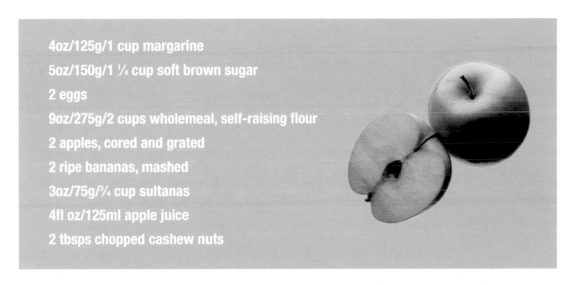

4oz/125g/1 cup margarine

5oz/150g/1 ¼ cup soft brown sugar

2 eggs

9oz/275g/2 cups wholemeal, self-raising flour

2 apples, cored and grated

2 ripe bananas, mashed

3oz/75g/¾ cup sultanas

4fl oz/125ml apple juice

2 tbsps chopped cashew nuts

1. Grease and line a shallow baking tin, 7 x 11 inches (18 x 28 cm). Preheat the oven to 18° C/350° F/Gas 4.
2. Beat the margarine and sugar together until light and fluffy. Beat in the eggs one at a time, adding a tablespoon of flour with the second egg.
3. Fold in half the remaining flour with the apples, bananas and sultanas.
4. Fold in the other half of the flour with the apple juice.
5. Turn the mixture into the tin and smooth the top. Bake for 45–50 minutes, until the cake springs back when lightly pressed.
6. Turn the cake out onto a wire rack to cool, then sprinkle with the chopped nuts. Cut into fingers.

relax

to energize

Life moves faster than ever. We juggle roles and change hats throughout the day – in just 24 hours, you could be a bread-winner, partner, parent, home-maker, son or daughter ... and now a fitness enthusiast as well!

In spite of all these jobs you already have – or maybe because of them – there's one more you need to do. Relax.

This is the one I actually find the hardest. I'm a manic do-er, always charging around getting things done. Jon enjoys watching TV in the evening after Fin has gone to bed but I have to force myself to sit down for half an hour. There's always something which needs to be done!

Luckily, athletics taught me that taking time to chill out is an important part of finding your personal best. Although I worked incredibly hard during my training sessions, the down-time in between was just as important. As well as rest-days during the week, when my body could recuperate and grow stronger, I always took six weeks off at the end of the year. Once all the big competitions were over and I'd demanded every ounce of myself, that was it – for the first three weeks, I could do anything, go any-where and eat whatever I liked. If I put on a stone, who cared? It was purely indulgent 'me' time. After four weeks my mind would start to wander back to training and at the end of six weeks – boy, I couldn't wait to get back into it! My mind and body were totally recharged and hungry for another season's achievements.

Now I'm a working mother, the timetable is different but the idea is still the same. Little chunks of time-out help me absorb whatever I've been doing and recharge me for the next bout. Like exercise, you don't need a huge stretch of time to do it – it could be five minutes in a morning, half an hour in the evening or a luxurious two hour stretch at the weekend.

I try to give myself a total of 30 minutes to an hour of sit-down time a day. If that means the dishwasher isn't emptied or the laundry doesn't go in the machine, tough.

why it's okay to relax

If you find it difficult to justify your sit-down and chill-out time, remember this:

1. Like fitness, relaxation is an investment. Would you rather take time out when it suits you, for how long it suits you, or have it forced upon you by exhaustion or illness?

2. When you feel relaxed, everyone benefits. I know Finley gets a better quality of mum when I'm re-energized, than when I'm tired and overstretched. Although relaxation time might mean time for you, it's not selfish time at all.

3. Amazing but true – five minutes of doing nothing gets your jobs done faster. If you close your eyes and breathe deeply for a few moments, you'll focus better on what you're doing now, instead of the six million things you have to do next.

4. Although our culture is body-focused, everything flows from your thoughts. If you use relaxation time to tap into your mind, it comes back with more ideas and solutions for your problems.

5. Life isn't a treadmill! Whatever you're living now, counts as life. The time you take to assess it, appreciate it and enjoy it will never be wasted.

what's the best way to relax?

Jon manages to plonk down in front of the television and that's it – he's relaxed. I wish I found it so easy. Although I enjoy a bit of telly I don't always find it totally relaxing. For one thing, there's the silent voices of all the other jobs I could be doing, for another, it can actually leave me feeling drained. Half an hour, an hour can whizz by without you even noticing; the whole evening vanishes and you don't have much to show for it.

I prefer 'active' ways to relax. Can you relax and be active at the same time? Definitely, as long as your activity is calming, peaceful and enjoyable. I find it very rewarding – as someone who finds it hard to sit still, it ensures I take time out without taxing my body or brain more than necessary.

relax to energize

155

The time you take to assess and appreciate life will never be wasted

These are some of my favourite forms of active relaxation. Others include playing with Fin, family walks and evenings out with friends, but these are things you can do on your own, whenever you feel the need.

yoga

I took up yoga when I was pregnant to help me relax and recharge my batteries. I go to a class in my local village with a friend; it's a good chance to catch up with her and the regular date ensures I block off the necessary time in my diary (and in my head).

It's very calming. Even if I'm frantic with things to do before the class, for the whole hour they vanish out of my mind. I just think about the poses; my brain has a well-earned rest and feels refreshed by the time I come out.

Most Western classes are based on Hatha yoga, which consists of gentle stretches held for a period of time, anything from 30 seconds to a couple of minutes. Under this umbrella there's a number of variations such as Kundalini, Bikram, Viniyoga and Iyengar. If your main goal is relaxation, ask the teacher how energetic a particular class is – some types, such as Ashtanga (also known as Power Yoga), are extremely demanding!

The moves in all types of Hatha yoga are called poses or postures (asanas), which realign the body. An integral part is breathing (pranayama) which helps your relaxation and focus, and sometimes meditation (dhyana). Some teachers include these as visualizations during the class, while some classes last an hour and a half and include time at the end to lie down and focus on breathing and visualization. The combination can leave you feeling totally renewed and ready to go.

You don't have to be incredibly flexible before you go – although this will improve with time, along with strength and endurance, you should perform the moves within your own limits. The less competitive and judgemental you are with your body, the more it will reward you by taking you further into the poses.

Over 84,000 asanas have developed over the last 5,000 years but I'm only going to show you one, short sequence, to give you a tiny taste of the types of beautiful, flowing poses you would learn from a regular yoga class. On its own, it's a wonderful thing to do first thing in the morning too. Take it gently and only stretch as far as comfortable.

SUN SALUTATION

I do this four or five mornings a week, as soon as I get out of bed. Once you learn the sequence, let it flow naturally, with just a few seconds' pause at each pose. Repeat 8 or 10 times to oxygenate your system and put your mind in touch with your body, ready for the day.

1. Stand tall with the palms of your hands together in front of your chest.

2. Inhale as you raise your arms and gently arch your back to stretch the front of your body. Tighten your buttocks to keep your back strong. Look straight up.

3. Exhale and bend forwards. Try to bend at the hips, rather than the waist, until your hands are on the mat beside your feet. Bend your knees if you need to – this gets easier over time.

4. Inhale and look up. Take your body weight on your hands and take a big step back with your right leg, so the top of your foot is in contact with the floor. (Your knee should not touch the floor.)

5. Hold your breath and take the left leg back to join the right leg, so your weight is now on your hands and the toes of both feet as though you were about to do a press up.

6. Exhale and lower your knees to the floor, then your forehead, chest and pelvis. Think caterpillar! Relax your feet.

7. Inhale and push up your upper body until your arms are nearly straight and your back is comfortably arched. Your hands should be directly beneath your shoulders. Don't over-stretch. Look up if you can. This position is called the Cobra.

8. Exhale and raise your hips by pushing against your hands. Your butt should make the highest point of an upside-down V. Aim to keep your feet flat on the floor (don't worry if you can't), your back and arms long, your head between your arms. This position is called Downward Dog.

Repeat the cycle

9. Inhale and bring your right leg forward, between your hands. It's the same position as step 4, but with the other leg back.

10. Exhale as you bring your other leg forward.

11. Inhale as you come up to a standing position and move smoothly into the backward bend of step 1.

12. Exhale and return to your start position, with palms together in front of your chest. Breathe slowly until you're ready to repeat the sequence.

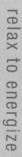

relax to energize

aromatherapy

Have you ever walked past a pine tree and thought of Christmas? Or a hay bale and thought of childhood picnics? Our sense of smell is so tightly connected with memory and emotion that just one whiff can send you straight back to another time and place, and make you feel as happy or sad as you did then.

Aromatherapists use the power of smell to help people relax, revive and heal their bodies. They use essential oils – aromatic essences extracted from plants, flowers, trees, fruit, bark, grasses and seeds.

I first tried aromatherapy when I heard it could help me relax before a big race. It can be very nerve wracking the night before you have to go out and show the world what you can do. The more I wanted a good night's sleep, the harder it was to unwind. I put a few drops of lavender oil in my bath and a few on a tissue, which I put in my pillow and guess what? I fell asleep easily.

Since then I've become a firm believer and use aromatherapy on a daily basis. Therapists say you reap the best rewards from an aromatherapy massage because essential oil molecules are so small they can be absorbed by the skin. I try to have one every couple of weeks and always leave feeling like a new woman, relaxed yet alert. I also swear by it for preventing illness, and always book a massage if I feel a cold coming on.

WHICH OIL SHOULD I CHOOSE?

There's only one rule for essential oils – buy the real thing. Synthetic oils never smell right to me, but more to the point, they just don't work. Look at the label of the bottle to see exactly what's in it; it should say 'essential oil' rather than 'room fragrance' or similar. Single oils such as 'lavender' or 'rose' usually come in a 5ml bottle with a dropper. Bigger bottles might have a mixture of essential oils blended for a special purpose, such as relaxation, and diluted with a carrier oil such as grapeseed or sweet almond oil; these are good for massage. The best oils are always more expensive but they last ages as you only need a few drops at a time. Besides, the cost is justifiable when you think it takes about eight million jasmine flowers, picked by hand at dawn, to make just 1kg of oil!

Each oil has its own, special properties. A therapist can mix and match oils to suit your mood, health concerns and preferences, but you're perfectly safe to explore along these guidelines:

Stimulating oils

When you lack energy or need concentration, try:

Lemon – also helps warts, acne and indigestion;
Peppermint – also helps muscle fatigue, bronchitis, travel sickness;
Rosemary – also helps colds, aches and pains, mental and muscular fatigue;
Basil, cardamom, ginger, thyme.

Relaxing oils

When you feel stressed or wound up, try:

Lavender – my all-time favourite, also helps headache, cystitis and skin problems;
Clary sage – also helps with menstrual problems;
Geranium – soothing yet refreshing; also helps with PMT, menopause and skin complaints;
Ylang ylang – relaxing yet euphoric, with aphrodisiac properties;
Chamomile, frankincense, jasmine, marjoram, rose, sandalwood.

Healing oils

Use these to help physical conditions:

Eucalyptus – antiseptic and decongestant, use for colds and chest infections;
Tea tree – antifungal and antiseptic, use for cuts, insect bites and dandruff;
Lavender – excellent for burns; helps minor cuts or insect bites;
Rosemary and thyme – both good for coughs, colds and infections.

HOW DO I USE THEM?

Baths

This is how I use aromatherapy every day. The heat of the water aids absorption; it's a fantastic way to unwind, take stock and prepare for a good night's sleep. Add up to eight drops of neat oil for adults, four for children over two years-old and stir in to your warm (not hot) bath.

Showers

If I'm pushed for time, just a few drops of neat oil on a sponge makes a shower more invigorating.

Massage

Great if you can persuade your partner to do it for you, otherwise you can do your own neck and shoulders. Use five drops of neat oil for every teaspoon of carrier oil, mix in a bowl, spread over warm hands and massage into the skin. For children under seven use half that strength and a quarter for children under three. It's best not to use essential oils on small babies. Try not to shower for at least an hour after your massage, so the oils can be absorbed.

Oil burners

Releases the scent into a room with a small ceramic bowl which sits over a flame. Heat a small amount of water and add a few drops of your favourite essence. Watch it doesn't burn dry. Alternatively, put a few drops of oil in a ceramic ring which can be warmed on a light bulb.

Inhalation

Put one or two drops of oil on a handkerchief and breathe them in wherever you go. Put a couple of drops of relaxing oil on a tissue and put it in your pillowcase to help you sleep. Steam inhalation is especially good for coughs or colds – breath from a bowl of steaming water with a few drops of eucalyptus, pine, lavender, black pepper, lemon or peppermint. Drape a towel over your head and around the bowl for maximum steam intake.

Compresses

For bruising, period pain and skin problems, add two drops to a bowl of warm water. Soak a flannel or piece of cotton wool in the water, squeeze it out and place it over the area needing treatment. Cover with a warm towel and leave as long as possible – at least two hours.

CAN THEY DO ANY HARM?

Essential oils are powerful and can cause irritation if put directly on the skin with two important exceptions: lavender oil, which is effective when used neat on burns, and tea tree oil, which has healing properties when dabbed on cuts, grazes, spots, bites and stings.

Always follow the instructions and use the recommended dosage. If you are pregnant, have an allergy, eczema, high blood pressure, epilepsy or other medical condition, check with a therapist before using them. Use on babies or young children only as directed.

facial massage

Stress and tension always goes straight to my neck and shoulders. Not only does that make painful knots of muscle, it brings me one step closer to a nasty tension headache – the last thing you need when you've got something important to achieve.

Before I resort to pills I always try to massage the tension away first. Applying gentle pressure to certain points on the face eases stress and encourages tiny muscles to relax. Just taking a few moments to close your eyes and focus on yourself also helps.

Before you start, wash and dry your hands. Then rub your palms together so they're warm and energy flows through them. Apply firm pressure through your fingertips, placing and pressing them rather than rubbing, especially on the delicate skin under the eyes and across the nose. Press each point for three to five seconds, and continue the massage for one to three minutes. Breathe deeply and calmly throughout.

the facial massage

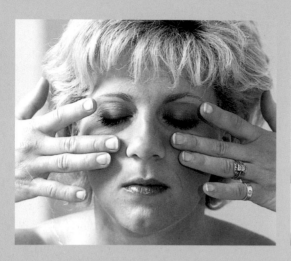

1. Begin with your middle fingers under your eyes. Find the bony ridge of your eye sockets and press along it, starting by your nose and moving out.

2. When you get to the temples, give them a gentle rub and push your fingers up, into your hair line.

3. Now place your fingertips so they meet in the middle of your forehead. Place and press out towards your temples, then repeat with a light, sweeping motion.

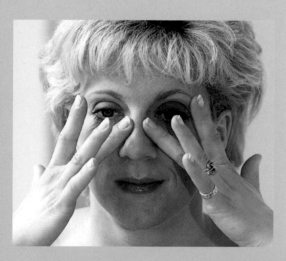

4. Return to the bridge of the nose. With your middle and index fingers, place and press down both sides of the nose and under your cheek bones. This is also very good for sinus trouble.

5. Finish by tapping your fingertips on your chin and across your jaw.

instant calmers

Here's some other ideas to help you wind down:

1. Breathe! It's so simple, yet many of us fail to do it properly. Breathing naturally becomes shallow when you're under stress, but habitual shallow breathing can make you feel stressed when there's no need. Learn the habit of breathing so deeply your abdomen rises as well as your chest.
2. Palming. Counteract eyestrain and reduce facial tension at your desk. Sit comfortably, rub your hands together to warm them and rest your elbows on the desk. Then cup your palms and place one over each eye. Shut your eyes and relax for a minute.
3. Inward focus. Sit comfortably, close your eyes and focus on your inner core. Try to switch off your chattering conscious mind; concentrate on the energy inside you. It may help to repeat an affirmation over and over, such as 'I am strong and capable' or 'I control my world'. Twenty minutes daily is wonderful but just five minutes can make a big difference whenever you need it
4. Head massage. This is a great way to release tension at any time (except if you've just been to a hairdresser!). Spread your fingertips and push them through your hair. Then rub, scrub and wiggle your scalp as though giving yourself a thorough shampoo, concentrating on any achy spots. You come out looking like a gorse bush but even this is a cheer-up!
5. If you have trouble sleeping, develop a bed-time ritual. Don't charge around until the last minute, then expect to drop off easily. Wind down for half an hour with a warm bath or shower and enjoy a few minute's bed-time reading or talking. Don't watch TV in bed as you'll give your brain the wrong signals. A warm, milky drink really helps (but not too much sugar).

be your

personal

best team:

how did they do?

After eight weeks on this programme, the Team was ready to reveal. They each did around three to four hours of exercise a week and made small changes to their eating habits and lifestyle – here's what they achieved.

Alison

New exercise routine:
Dumbbell weights routine, abdominal exercises and stretches three times a week; one hour's inline skating along the local sea front once a week.

New eating habits:
I have cut down on chocolate! From five bars a day to just two. I tried to keep myself busy when I'd normally stop and snack and didn't miss it much. I also have a fruit bowl and help myself throughout the day, especially on nectarines and bananas.

I drink a lot more water and have cut coffee from eight cups a day to two or three.

Best achievement:
Learning to inline skate. I dug out the pair I bought ages ago and asked a friend to teach me how to use them. I don't do anything clever, just go in a straight line but it's really fun, and harder than I expected. I can feel my bum and thighs working hard even though it counts as aerobic exercise. Going out in public was difficult at first because little kids whizz past all the time but the other day I passed a woman who could hardly stand up, which made me feel quite good! I love being by the sea and there's a long promenade which takes half an hour each way.

Any difficulties?
Fitting the weights in when I'm busy but I always do them three times a week, even if I have to split it into a morning and evening session. It only takes half an hour in total – I know I can always find that much time.

Overall result:
I feel much fitter and healthier. I have a lot more energy and can run to the end of the yard without being out of breath, which used to knacker me. Friends say I look fitter even though my weight is the same. My arms look quite muscley and I'm using heavier weights than I did to start with.

I'll definitely carry on. I couldn't squeeze in another session but that doesn't matter – I feel really good with what I'm doing.

Lucy

New exercise routine:
Dumbbell weights routine twice a week, resistance bands once a week. Running for up to 40 minutes three times a week, plus dog-walking daily.

New eating habits:
I'm much more careful with my business lunches. I choose things like grilled fish or chicken salad, and if I really feel like pasta I'll have it with a tomato sauce. Usually I manage to skip pudding and have cappuccino but if not, I go for a sorbet or something with fruit, so I at least get some vitamins from it. In the evening I ask myself if I really am hungry after that big lunch and adjust my portions accordingly.

I've given up biscuits and don't even buy cakes. We still have crisps and alcohol, but only at the weekend.

Best achievement:
Building up my weights routine. I'm impressed how effective it is – I've benefited at least as much as I did at the gym. I also find it easier to focus, because at the gym you can wander aimlessly from machine to machine. I find the resistance bands really good, especially for the legs. It's a great compromise.

I've also cranked up my running from once to three times a week and now go 10–15 minutes longer than I used to. Once a week I try to go slightly faster than my normal pace and that's a definite challenge.

Any difficulties?
Just fitting everything in. It's not easy but I decided to stick it out no matter what and I get really mad at myself if I slip. It's a mind-set really – you just have to give it a priority.

Overall result:
I'm definitely more toned, especially my arms. My self-esteem has improved and my exercise is more focused. I'm really pleased that you don't have to go to the gym to keep in shape.

Karen

New exercise routine:

Resistance band routine once or twice a week; abdominal exercises for 20 minutes every second night. Running for 25 minutes, three times a week.

New eating habits:

I've made a conscious effort not to eat the children's food and scrape left-overs into the bin. I've gone from six cups of tea (with sugar) a day to none, replacing them with cold water and Sally's hot water drink with lemon and honey.

Best achievement:

A three mile road race! It was incredibly hard but I finished in 35 minutes. I felt wonderful afterwards, tired but so pleased to have done something I'd never expected.

I've discovered I really enjoy running. At first I could only go for five or 10 minutes, then I'd walk briskly before running a bit more. Now I can run for 20 minutes without stopping. I asked Ryan to come out with me when I started because I thought everyone would look at me and think, 'Oh look, she's a beginner.' Now I know no-one takes any notice and I feel so free. I drop the kids at my mum's house and value it as time for me.

Any difficulties?

Doing the resistance exercises at home. I'm good at exercising when I have to go out but I haven't got the right mental attitude to do it at home. I can only do them in the evening, after the kids have gone to bed so maybe I'm tired as well. It helps if Ryan does them with me.

Overall result:

A few items of clothing fit me better but the biggest difference is my energy. I don't crawl off to bed at 9pm any more, I can stick it until 11. It's the running I'm most enthusiastic about – I now want to do a five mile event.

Neil

New exercise routine:

Weights three times a week, twice at the gym, once at home. Aerobic work such as running, stepping or rowing in the gym twice a week for 20 minutes each time, plus running or cycling at the weekends.

New eating habits:

I eat a lot more fruit and vegetables but I was basically happy with my diet and haven't made any big changes. I try to eat only what's on my plate though, rather than polish off other people's left-overs.

Best achievement:

Although I've been to a gym off-and-on for many years, this is the first time I've enjoyed weights. I used to do the things which made me sweat the most like the treadmill, but I've really felt the benefit of working with dumbbells. I've also learned to use a skipping rope – it's excellent aerobic work for a Sunday morning. After 15 minutes I'm drenched.

Any difficulties?

It has been a struggle to fit it all in. On Monday morning I might decide to go to the gym on Tuesday and Thursday but if I'm busy at work I put it off. Sometimes it gets to Friday and I realise I have to go or I won't have been all week! So although twice a week is ideal, I've probably only managed it 50 per cent of the time. The only way around it is to be firm with myself and say, well, I've just got to do it. I find that easier at weekends and make a point of doing something on Sunday mornings. My wife does the weights routine with me and the kids find it highly amusing – it's very challenging to do crunches with two of them sitting on you.

Overall result:

My aerobic capacity has improved thanks to the extra gym sessions. I feel much stronger and more toned around my arms, which is very satisfying. I still have excess girth which makes me wonder if I will have to look at my diet more carefully but overall I've developed a new awareness which should help me keep it up.

New exercise routine:

Weights and abdominal exercises three or four times a week, mixing resistance bands at home and dumbbells at the gym. Cycling to work three times a week in an eight mile round trip.

New eating habits:

No more biscuits! I used to have them all the time at work; in the first week of the programme I just stopped. I didn't miss them at all and realized it was just a habit. I can't remember the last time I had chocolate; I eat masses of fruit instead.

I've reduced the size of my meals. I used to have quite big portions but found I feel better if I'm not so full.

I drink a lot more water and only three cups of tea a day plus a very rare coffee if we go out.

Best achievement:

I won a doubles tournament at tennis, which wasn't bad going! I won one years ago but this was a bit of a novelty. I've got more energy so I can run around more to get to balls and hit them better because I'm stronger.

I'm also pleased with my cycling. I bought a new bike and thoroughly enjoy the ride to work. I know exactly how long the journey is going to take, which you never know in the car – it's about 20 minutes each way. I choose quiet roads and there's cycle paths for half the trip, so the traffic doesn't worry me. I only skip it if it's pouring with rain.

Any difficulties?

Sometimes the weights are a bit boring – it's much more appealing to sit down and read a book. I just tell myself it's making me feel better and doing me good, and I listen to music while I work out.

Overall result:

I've lost half a stone and feel healthier and more energetic. The upper body weights have definitely made a difference – my muscles feel more toned and the exercises have become easier. I'll persevere because the more you do the better you feel, and I think that's especially important as you get older.

annual events

Signing up for an event is a terrific motivator. Here's some of the nation's best to whet your appetite:

EVENTS FOR WOMEN

FLORA LIGHT CHALLENGE FOR WOMEN
3 miles (5k) run or walk with more than 12,000 participants.
July; Hyde Park, London
020 7902 0189; www.london-marathon.co.uk

RACE FOR LIFE
3 miles (5k) run or walk – there's sure to be one near you! Women only; raises funds for Imperial Cancer Research Fund.
May – July; 62 locations nationwide
08705 134 314; www.icnet.uk/raceforlife

DUBLIN WOMEN'S MINIMARATHON
10k road race famous for its brilliant atmosphere; over 33,000 women take part.
June; Dublin, Ireland
00 353 1 496 0838; womensminimarathon@circom.net

WOMEN'S LONDON RUN
10k road race; a challenging distance on a course which includes scenic Tower Bridge.
September; South East London
020 7252 1082

MOON WALK
Marathon and half-marathon power walk at night in a Wonderbra for Breakthrough Breast Cancer event. The biggest power walking event in the world! Amazing atmosphere, tough challenge.
May; London
01483 291472

RUNNING EVENTS

LESS THAN 10k

CAPITAL ONE FUN RUN
2.5 mile run which is part of the Experian Robin Hood Marathon event.
September; Nottingham
www.robinhoodmarathon.co.uk

CHASE CORPORATE CHALLENGE
3.5 miles on a fun, twisty course with a corporate edge – prize for first male and female CEOs!
July; Battersea Park, London
020 7902 0189; www.london-marathon.co.uk

ELDERSFIELD BEER RACE
A family day out with a 4.2 mile run and beer to all finishers!
May; Eldersfield, Gloucester
28 Avebury Close, Tuffley, GL4 0TS

ASICS ALSAGER 5
800+ runners on a 5 mile route; locals turn up to cheer.
February; near Crewe
01782 330 853

WESTON PROM RUNS
A flat 5 miles along the promenade.
Jan, Feb, March, April; Weston Sea Front, Somerset
Dave Jones, 93 Spring Hill, Worle, Weston-Super-Mare, BS22 9BB

NIKE BLAYDON RACE
A wild evening out, running 5.7 miles from the hedonistic Bigg Market to Blaydon.
June; Newcastle-upon-Tyne
Dr J Dewar, 72 Trajan Walk, Heddon on the Wall, NE15 0BL

10k RUNS

FILA/RUNNING FITNESS AUCKLAND CASTLE 10K
A 4k lap followed by a 6k lap and over 1,000 entrants.
October; Auckland Castle, County Durham
Julie Bowes, Leisure and Marketing Dept, Wear Valley District Council, Civic Centre, Crook, DL15 9ES.

PUMA 10k AT DEWSBURY
A fast, city centre course which is 5k uphill out of town, then back down.
February; Dewsbury, West Yorkshire
Bernard Disken, 13 Mitchell Ave, Dewsbury WF13 4JF

10 MILE RUNS

MIZUNO EREWASH 10 MILE CLASSIC
A scenic, rural route, though not the flattest of courses.
August; Sandiacre, Derbyshire
Terry Lines, 21 Ruskin Ave, Long Eaton NG10 3LD

NIKE BALLYCOTTON 10
10 miles of Irish hospitality and atmosphere, free tea and biscuits at the end. No hills.
March; Ballycotton, Co Cork
00 353 21 646 064

NEW FOREST 10
10 mile road and track race makes a family day out in the heart of beautiful forest.
July; New Park Farm, Brockenhurst, Hampshire
www.nf10.freeserve.co.uk

HALF MARATHONS (13.1 MILES)

BUPA GREAT NORTH RUN
The world's biggest half marathon, with 40,000 participants.
October; Newcastle-upon-Tyne to South Shields, Tyne and Wear
01538 702100; www.greatnorthrun.co.uk

be your best

LIVERPOOL INTERNATIONAL HALF MARATHON
Over 2,000 runners on a pleasant route with lots of buzz.
August; Sefton Park, Liverpool
runliverpool.org.uk

CITY OF NORWICH HALF MARATHON
A rural and flat course.
June; Norwich, Norfolk
www.conac.org.uk

YELLOW PAGES READING HALF MARATHON
A huge affair, taking 6,500+ runners around Reading.
March; Reading, Berkshire
0118 939 0771; www.yell.co.uk/halfmarathon

FILA HASTINGS HALF MARATHON
A hilly first six miles, then flat or downhill to finish on the sea front.
March; Hastings
01424 437001; eric.hardwich@greenvale.co.uk

LAKE VYRNWY HALF MARATHON
Very scenic run around a lake, fairly flat on quiet or closed roads.
September; Llanwddyn Village, North Powys
Doug Morris, 27 Whittington Rd, Oswestry, SY11 1JD

ALLSPORTS WILMSLOW HALF MARATHON
A scenic, rural race with 3,000 runners.
March; Wilmslow, Cheshire
10 Haddon Close, Macclesfield, SK11 7YG

DML/EUROBELL PLYMOUTH HALF MARATHON
Flat and scenic, with over 1,700 entrants.
May; Plymouth
Nigel Rowe, DML Sports and Social Club PC101, Devonport Dockyard, Plymouth PL1 4SG

ELLESMERE PORT HALF MARATHON
Explore 13.1 miles of residential and industrial Ellesmere; includes a couple of long, gentle gradients.
July; Ellesmere Port, Cheshire
www.rivacre-runners.org.uk

REEBOK HADDINGTON HALF MARATHON
A scenic and friendly 13.1 mile road race.
August; Haddington, East Lothian
Joe Forte Sports, 01620 824023

EVENTS WITH HALF (13.1 MILE) OR FULL (26.2 MILE)

MARATHON OPTIONS

EXPERIAN ROBIN HOOD MARATHON
A friendly event through historic Nottingham.
September; Nottingham
www.robinhoodmarathon.co.uk

do it! directory

175

WESTFIELD HEALTH SCHEME SHEFFIELD MARATHON AND HALF
Over 2,000 runners; out and back for the half marathon, two laps for the full.
April; Sheffield
www.ukco.co.uk/sheffield.marathon

PEPSI MAX KINGSTON MARATHON & HALF MARATHON
Pick your distance – 26, 16, 13 or 8 miles on a flat course.
October; Kingston, Surrey
020 8399 3579; www.humanrace.co.uk

20 MILE RUNS

TAYLOR ENGALL BURY 20
Scenic and rural 20 miles on quiet, undulating roads, 1,000+ runners.
February; Bury St Edmonds
CW Austin, 16 Flemyng Rd, Bury St Edmonds, IP33 7UZ

MARATHON (26.2 MILE) EVENTS

BELFAST CITY MARATHON
Pleasant route passes parks and historic buildings; 5,000 participants.
May; Belfast
Community & Leisure Services, Belfast City Council, 4–11 Linenhall St, Belfast BT2 8BP

MANCHESTER MARATHON
Route is designed to go past as many parks as possible.
October; Manchester City, Merseyside
www.manchester.gov.uk

STEELITE INTERNATIONAL POTTERIES MARATHON
An urban loop passing many pubs, so lots of support from the crowds.
June; Trentham Gardens, Stoke on Trent
Don Shelley, Marathon Office, Lichfield St, Stone, ST15 8NA

MOTHER'S PRIDE GREAT SCOTTISH RUN
A distinctly Scottish marathon, with a piper to mark each mile. Up to 12,000 entrants.
August; Glasgow
0141 248 9909

FLORA LONDON MARATHON
More than 30,000 entrants enjoy the carnival atmosphere of this famous event.
April; London
020 7902 0189; www.london-marathon.co.uk

GYM/SWIM EVENTS

BT SWIMATHON
Sponsored swims, 1,500m, 2,500m, 5,000m or as far as you like. You can set your own goals and swim at your own pace, solo or as a team.
March; nationwide
0800 731 7316 or watch for posters at swimming pools

GREAT BRITISH SWIM (ASTHMA CAMPAIGN)
Swim as far as possible, adding to a national total of 6,629 miles (equivalent to the UK coastline).
October; nationwide
020 7704 5861

be your best

PERPETUAL INDOOR ROWING CHAMPIONSHIPS
Go for your 2,000m personal best on a Concept II indoor rowing machine. All ages and abilities take part.
November; NEC, Birmingham
0115 945 5522; www.concept2.co.uk

XZONE
Compete against yourself in this gym-based cross-training competition. Choose either beginner, intermediate or advanced level, and test yourself when you're ready. Register a top time and go through to the final.
January – May; in your own gym, with a final near Birmingham
020 7928 5055; www.xzone.org.uk

MULTI-SPORT EVENTS

LONDON TRIATHLON
Sprint or Olympic distances combining swim, bike and run. Big event with competitors ranging from first timers to elite on a relatively flat course. Wet-suit needed.
Late September/early October; Docklands, London
020 7928 5055; www.thc-london-triathlon.org.uk

PEPSI MAX ROYAL WINDSOR TRIATHLON
Sprint or Olympic distances combining swim, bike and run. Huge event with a historical course around Eton, Windsor Castle and the Thames.
Wet-suit needed.
June; Windsor, Berkshire
020 8399 3579; www.humanrace.co.uk

HI-TEC ADVENTURE RACING SERIES
Cross-country triathlons with surprise challenges. A fun and challenging test for teams of three, taking 2–4 hours.
May–September; various locations in the UK
01538 703203; www.hi-tecadventureracingseries.co.uk

SALOMON ONE DAY X-ADVENTURE SERIES
Team challenge involving running, mountain biking, canoeing or rowing and usually an abseil. Testing but fun; six hours to find up to 17 checkpoints, but you only do as many as you want.
May–August; various locations in the UK
0800 389 4350; gb_events@salomon-sports.co.uk.

ACE RACES
A series of weekend adventure races including fell running, kayaking, night navigation. Exciting races but you need to be thoroughly prepared.
March–September; Forest of Dean, Snowdonia, Yorkshire, Lake District.
www.aceraces.demon.co.uk

CYCLING EVENTS

BRITISH HEART FOUNDATION LONDON TO BRIGHTON BIKE RIDE
A 58-mile bike ride involving 27,000 people and lots of families. They take a few hours to a whole day.
June; Clapham Common to Brighton
0891 616077; www.cycle-rides.co.uk

POLARIS CHALLENGE
Two day orienteering event on mountain bikes in teams of two on outback terrain. It's big, tough and very rough.
March, July, October; various locations in the UK.
www.polaris-apparel.co.uk

activity contacts

If you want to try a new activity, these organizations can point you in the right direction:

ARCHERY
Grand National Archery Society
01952 677888; www.gnas.org

ATHLETICS
UK Athletics
0121 456 5098; www.ukathletics.org

BADMINTON
Badminton Association of England
01908 268400; www.baofe.co.uk

BASEBALL
BaseballSoftballUK
020 7453 7055; www.baseballsoftballuk.com

BASKETBALL
English Basketball Association
0113 236 1166; www.basketballengland.org.uk

BOWLS
English Bowling Association
01903 820222; www.bowlsengland.com

BOXING
Amateur Boxing Association of England Ltd
020 8778 0251;
www.amateurboxing.freeserve.co.uk

CANOEING & KAYAKING
British Canoe Union
0115 982 1100; www.bcu.org.uk

CLAY PIGEON SHOOTING
Clay Pigeon Shooting Association
01536 443566; www.cpsa.co.uk

CONSERVATION WORK
BTCV
01491 821600; www.btcv.org
Can help you find a conservation holiday or local project to help with.

CROQUET
The Croquet Association
020 7736 3148; www.croquet.org.uk

CYCLING
British Cycling Federation
0161 2302301; www.bcf.uk.com
Can put you in touch with coaches for road, mountain, track and BMX cycling.

London Cycling Campaign
020 7928 7220; www.lcc.org.uk
Lots of help for Londoners wanting to cycle for transport.

DANCING
The British Dance Council
020 8545 0085; www.british-dance-council.org

Central Council of Physical Recreation
020 828 3163

Ceroc Enterprises
020 8846 8563; www.ceroc.com

English folk dancing
English Folk Dance and Song Society
020 7485 2206; www.efdss.org

Scottish country dancing
Royal Scottish Country Dance Society
0131 225 3854; www.rscds.org

FENCING
British Fencing Association
020 8742 3032; www.britishfencing.com

FOOTBALL
The Football Association
020 7262 4542; www.the-fa.org
Can give you the contact for your county FA.

GOLF
English Golf Union
01526 354500; www.englishgolfunion.org

HIKING
The Ramblers' Association
020 7339 8500; www.ramblers.org.uk
Network of walking groups which organise regular hikes of varying lengths. Guidebooks and information books available.

HOCKEY
English Hockey Association
01908 544644; www.hockeyonline.co.ukHang gliding

be your best

178

HORSE RIDING
British Horse Society
01926 707700; www.bhs.org.uk

ICE SKATING
National Ice Skating Association of UK Ltd
020 7613 1188; www.iceskating.org.uk

MARTIAL ARTS
Martial Arts Foundation
020 7405 0345; www.martialartsfoundation.org
Can suggest teachers or classes in most types of martial arts.

Amateur Martial Arts Association
020 7837 4406

Britich Council of Chinese Martial Arts
01203 394642; www.bccma.org.uk

British Aikido Board
01753 577878; www.bab.org.uk

British Judo Association
0116 255 9669; www.britishjudo.org.uk

British Ju-Jitsu Association Governing Body
0114 266 6733; www.kyushin-ryu.demon.co.uk/bjfilel.htm
English Karate Governing Body
01302 337645; www.ekgb.org.uk

British Kendo Association
020 7515 8653;
www.users.dircon.co.uk/bka~/index.htm
British Tae Kwon Do Council
0117 955 1046

Independent Tai Chi Association
07000 824244; energytraining.com

NETBALL
All England Netball Association
01462 442344; www.england-netball.co.uk

ORIENTEERING
British Orienteering Federation
01629 734 042; www.britishorienteering.org.uk

PARAGLIDING
British Hang Gliding and Paragliding Association
0116 261 1322; www.bhpa.co.uk

PILATES
The Pilates Foundation
07071 781 8559; www.pilatesfoundation.com

POWER WALKING
Walk the Walk
01483 291472; www.walkthewalk.org

Organizes powerwalking events for breast cancer; sign up for an event and you'll get a booklet and advice on walking for fitness.

ROCK CLIMBING (INDOOR & OUTDOOR)
British Mountaineering Council
0161 445 4747; www.thebmc.co.uk

ROWING
Amateur Rowing Association
020 8748 3632; www.ara-rowing.org

SAILING
Royal Yachting Association
02380 627400; www.rya.org.uk

SKIING
English Ski Council
0121 501 2314
Has a list of dry ski slopes in the UK.
Ski Club of Great Britain
020 8410 2000; www.skiclub.co.uk
Broad range of information, including resorts and holidays.

SKY DIVING
British Parachute Association
0116 278 5271; www.bpa.org.uk

SQUASH
The Squash Racquets Association
0161 231 4499; www.squash.co.uk

SUB-AQUA DIVING
British Sub-Aqua Club
0151 350 6200; www.bsac.com

PADI
0117 300 7234; www.padi.com

SURFING
British Surfing Association
01736 360250; www.britsurf.co.uk

SWIMMING
Amateur Swimming Association
01509 618700; www.swimming.org
Can help you find a swimming or diving club.
Institute of Swimming Teachers and Coaches
01509 264357; www.swimming.org.uk
Can help you find a teacher.

TENNIS
Lawn Tennis Association
020 7381 7111; www.lta.org.uk/playtennis

TRIATHLON
British Triathlon Association
01530 414234; www.britishtriathlon.co.uk

do it! directory

179

VOLLEYBALL
English Volleyball Association
0115 981 6324;
http://members.netscapeonline.co.uk/chasvolleyball

WATER SKIING
British Water Ski Federation
020 7833 2855; bwsf.co.uk

WINDSURFING
Royal Yachting Association
02380 627400; www.rya.org.uk

YOGA
British Wheel of Yoga
01529 306851; www.bwy.org.uk
Governing body; can direct you to a teacher of
Hatha yoga.

The Life Centre
020 7221 4602; www.yoga.co.uk
Teachers of Ashtanga yoga.

Iyengar Yoga Institute
020 7624 3080; www.iyi.org.uk
Teachers of Iyengar yoga.

Bikram's Yoga College of India
020 7692 6900; www.bikramyoga.com
Teachers of Bikram yoga.

NATIONAL MOUNTAIN CENTRES
These offer tuition to all ages and abilities in a full
range of outdoor activities, from beginner rock
climbing to mountain leadership:
Glenmore Lodge in Scotland (01479 861256)
Plas Y Brenin in North Wales (01690 720214)
Tollymore Mountain Centre in Northern Ireland
(028 4372 2158).

inspiration

Check these websites for useful information and advice:

www.hfonline.co.uk
Fitness test, running workout plus news, tips and information from Health & Fitness magazine.

www.adventuredirectory.com
Whatever you want to try, anywhere in the country (or world!), this directory will point you to holiday and activity operators.

www.primusweb.com/fitnesspartner
Unbiased, well-researched advice from certified trainers on improving your routine, sports injuries and other fitness concerns.

www.drkoop.com/wellness/fitness
Includes 'Four Get Fit' feature, where you can follow the progress of four new exercisers.

www.sweatybetty.com
Interactive fitness questionnaire, ideas for fitness activities, advice on fitness clothing and fabrics from Sweaty Betty sportswear retailers for women.